FASTBREAK

THE CEO'S GUIDE
TO STRATEGY EXECUTION

(SECOND EDITION)

JOHN R. CHILDRESS

PRINCIPIA
ASSOCIATES

First edition published in November 2012
Second edition published by The Principia Group in
November 2013.

The Principia Group
27 Brook Green
London W6 7BL
ISBN: 9780957517981

Printed by Lightning Source Lightning Source UK Ltd.

For speaking engagements, consulting, or other business
matters, contact:
John R Childress, Managing Partner, The Principia Group
john@johnrchildress.com
www.businessbooks.johnrchildress.com

There is no strategy without execution,
and there is no execution without leadership.
~ John R. Childress

TABLE OF CONTENTS

How This Book Is Organized   3

Introduction   5

Section One: Welcome to the Hot Seat!   7
Chapter 1: Execution is the Competitive Advantage   21
Chapter 2: The Opportunity   25
Chapter 3: The CEO's Lament: Execution, Execution, Execution 31
Chapter 4: Sleeping Policemen and other barriers to Strategy
Execution   37
Chapter 5: Disconnected Initiatives and Project Overload   53
Chapter 6: Silos are Geat for Missiles, but not for
Organizations   57

Section Two: What's the Plan, Stan?   61
Chapter 7: The Need for Speed   63
Chapter 8: Introducing the Strategy-on-a-Page-Excecution
Roadmap   67
Chapter 9: A Real 'Roadmap'   77

Section Three: Building your Strategy-on-a-Page
Execution Roadmap   81
Chapter 10: I Want . . .   87
Chapter 11: How do We Make Money?   93
Chapter 12: The Big Hairy Monster and Limiting Factor(s)   95
Chapter 13: The Necessary Foundation for Competitive Combat 101
Chapter 14: Talk is Cheap, so are Value Statements - Focus on
Behaviors and Ground Rules Instead   107
Chapter 15: The Target - Clear and Simple   113
Chapter 16: Single Malt Scotch and Breakthrough Thinking   117
Chapter 17: Strategy as a Balancing Act   123
Chapter 18: Strategic Initiatives - Where the Rubber Meets the
Road   131

Chapter 19: Kill all the Pets!   141
Chapter 20: KPIs - What Gets Measured Gets Delivered   145
Chapter 21: The Prize - Enterprise Metrics   153

Section Four: Hanging Together or Hanging Together   157
Chapter 22: Strategic Leadership and Aligment   159
Chapter 23: Who's on First, What's on Second? . . .
Roles and Responsibilities   183
Chapter 24: Culture Matters, Big Time   189

Section Five: Execution, Execution, Execution   195
Chapter 25: Cadence - Regular Strategy Review Meetings   199
Chapter 26: Dealing with 'Breakdowns'   205
Chapter 27: Frog in a Rut and Effective Strategy Execution   207

Section Six: Building Critical Mass   213
Chapter 28: Communication, Employee Engagement and
Innovation   217

Section Seven: Q&A about Fastbreak Strategy
Execution   225

Section Eight: Run Like Hell!   231
Chapter 29:" Once More Unto the Breach, Dear Friends!"
 - The Annual Planning Cycle   233

Conclusion, but not the End   237

Acknowledgments   239

About the Author   243

About The Principia Group   245

Citations   247

Bibliography   250

How This Book Is Organized

*The secret of all victory lies in the organization of
the non-obvious. ~ Marcus Aurelius*

I have chosen to organize this as a guidebook, in Sections. Each section tackles one of the big issues of effective strategy execution, so you can read straight through, or skip around to the areas you feel are most appropriate. Inside each section are various chapters. All the chapters are purposefully short and only touch on the key elements. Again, this is not an academic treatise, but a guidebook to help you get the most out of your strategy journey. I have also included numerous links and citations to material and readings that go into much more depth and provide added background and insights. Follow them as you choose.

INTRODUCTION

When I was in high school in the 1960s, I played Junior Varsity basketball my freshman year. It was 1962 to be exact, and my one and only basketball season. I started out being the same height as most of my teammates and ended the season as one of the smallest. Needless to say I didn't win the genetic lottery for height. Most games I sat on the bench and cheered.

But that one basketball season left a profound impression that has stuck with me throughout my professional and business career. Our coach was a master of the 'fast break.' Basically, a fast break is a departure from the traditional cadence of play, which can best be described as: gain control of the ball, dribble slowly down towards the basket, allowing your teammates to get in position, then pass the ball back and forth while looking for an opening in the defense in order to score.

A 'fast break', on the other hand, goes like this: get the rebound or the inbound ball, quickly throw it down the court to one or two teammates who have sprinted ahead of the defenders, and score two points. The opposing team is caught flat-footed, you've added a quick score, and the defense is unnerved since there is no real way to defend against the fast break. It's an unexpected, quick strike. Whenever we needed a lift during the game or were on the verge of being outplayed, coach would get us into fast break mode. More often than not it turned the tide of the game in our favor.

Fast forward 15 years and I am the co-founder of an international consulting firm watching executive teams ponderously execute on their strategic plans, most based on previous year plans. In those days, a 10% improvement was considered breakthrough.

But occasionally I would get to work with a fired up, hard charging, come-from-behind organization full of hungry go-getters. Usually they were in an exploding new industry, like global telecoms, specialty retail or computer manufacturing. They were not bound to the past or traditional ways of doing business. They were looking for competitive advantages anywhere they could find them, and speed was their mantra. Double-digit growth was the ticket to entry and winning took every ounce of innovation, motivation, teamwork and courage the management team could muster.

It was during this time that we began developing various consulting processes for rapid change and business transformation. And since change was in the air (beginning with the deregulation of the telecommunications industry in the US, growing into globalization and accelerating as the digital revolution), our focus on leadership, culture and senior team alignment helped many companies thrive and survive.

The experience and insights gained from my 35-year journey in working with senior executive teams during times of transition are the basis for this guidebook.

SECTION ONE:
WELCOME TO THE HOT SEAT!

*To every person there comes in their lifetime that special
moment when they are figuratively tapped on the
shoulder and offered the chance to do a very special
thing, unique to them and fitted to their talents. What a
tragedy if that moment finds them unprepared or
unqualified for the work which could be their finest hour.*
~ Winston Churchill

The headline of the June 21, 1999 issue of *Fortune Magazine*[1]
screamed the words: 'Why CEOs Fail.' Ram Charan and Geoffrey
Colvin studied over 40 failed CEOs from Fortune 500 companies to
see what went wrong. The fatal flaw of these failed CEOs was
pretty simple: poor execution. Charan and Colvin summarized
their article this way, *"They were all smart people who worried
deeply about a lot of things. They just weren't worrying enough
about the right things: execution, decisiveness, follow-through,
delivering on commitments."*

That was over a decade ago. What about today? A 2012 article in *Forbes Magazine*[2] has this to say:

> ... *CEO failures are even more visible than they were 13 years ago — and in high definition. Last year alone, the CEOs of British Petroleum, Hewlett-Packard, Burger King, Bank of New York Mellon and Yahoo were unceremoniously shown the door for failures that—in addition to lackluster execution—also included poor communications skills, an abrasive management style and the wholesale defection of unhappy executives.*
>
> *Execution is as critical as ever, in and of itself, but today we also have transparency to deal with ... no matter what the level. The CEO is communicating with his every move and—because of the open window into our business that has been enabled by the Internet—stakeholders are learning about poor CEO execution faster.*

The July 2003 issue of the *Harvard Business Review* reported on a 10-year study of 160 companies and their total shareholder returns[3]. In every case, companies that outperformed their industry peers excelled in four main management practices—strategy, execution, culture and organization. Again we find the importance of execution in business success.

And today we find a classic case of poor execution at RIM (Research in Motion – the Blackberry guys) where they are consistently unable to launch new products to keep up with the growing competition from iPhone and Androids. In fact RIM can't even launch new products as fast as they used to!

How is your company's track record on execution? Are you long on plans and PowerPoint decks but short on results? What is the level of confidence among middle management and supervisors (where real work gets done) about being able to deliver on a major change program or aggressive set of business objectives?

A recent research study[4] of over 400 companies found that 49% of the leaders reported a gap between their organization's ability to formulate a strategy and its ability to deliver results. Shockingly, only 36% of the leaders in companies with an execution gap had confidence in their organization's ability to close the gap!

On the other hand, there have also been some spectacular demonstrations of execution. How did Gordon Bethune and Greg Brenneman orchestrate the massive turnaround of Continental Airlines, with 40,000 employees, in one year (1994-1995) from being $2.5 billion in default and having 10 years of successive losses to a $200+ million profit in 1995 and leading the global airline league tables for the next 10 years?[5]

How have Alan Mulally, Lewis Booth and the senior team of Ford Motor Company, without bailout money from the US government, engineered a massive turnaround in profitability, market share and customer satisfaction?[6]

How did Bill McLaughlin, a former senior executive from PepsiCo, take a failing mattress manufacturer, 'Sleep Comfort, and build it into a nation-wide business with high growth, excellent profits and raving customers? [7] [8]

The answer lies in two ingredients that are rarely thought of as interrelated: STRATEGY and EXECUTION.

What is FASTBREAK Strategy Execution?

The **FASTBREAK Strategy Execution** process is a unique combination of leadership alignment, culture change and performance management, led by the senior team, that seamlessly combines both hard and soft skills (head and heart, process analytics and human psychology) into a robust and effective process for delivering business results. A significant element of the **FASTBREAK Strategy Execution** process is the Strategy-on-a-Page Execution Roadmap, where the entire business strategy is visually presented in a line-of-sight approach with objectives linking to initiatives linking to metrics linking to performance outcomes. As you will discover in this book, it is a powerful approach to strategy execution.

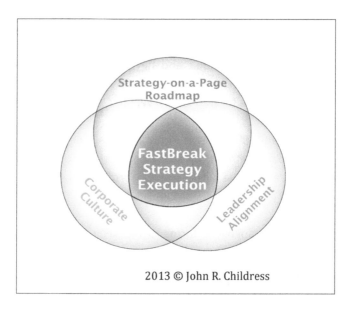

Strategy-on-a-Page Roadmap

FastBreak Strategy Execution

Corporate Culture

Leadership Alignment

2013 © John R. Childress

Why this book?

What if... you could get all your employees fully engaged (hearts & minds) in the delivery of key business outcomes and have the delivery driven by a robust methodology and process architecture of defined accountabilities, management discipline and governance?

In this day and age of global financial upheaval, exploding competition from all corners, and with the Internet, social media and technology enabling radically new business models, it is easy to get depressed about your business prospects. The previous decades of buoyant markets and easy money are long gone and everywhere companies are struggling to remain viable and find new ways to win. Everywhere you turn there is bad news.

But the opportunity for those who can find a way through is huge. Massive new markets are opening up, thirsty for goods and services. Technological advances are bringing about whole new industries and along with them, whole new business opportunities.

The prevailing wisdom (or rather the current dogma) is that strategy is strategy, and execution is execution. This has been popularized in the much-used phrase: *'A poor strategy executed well is better than an excellent strategy poorly executed.'* I don't buy that simplistic notion. Strategy and execution are inseparable; distinct but intimately interconnected, much like the two sides of a coin. They don't work when separated.

There is no strategy without execution.

There are binders, there are charts, there are spreadsheets and forecasts, and huge consultant invoices, but there is no strategy unless there is also execution. We see strategy as a living organism that only expresses itself though the process of being delivered. A 50-deck PowerPoint presentation of the strategy may impress the board of directors, but it won't impress the competition or angry customers. Execution is the only competitive advantage. Strategy can only be realized through execution.

Strategy is not static; something that first gets developed and then gets implemented, precisely as laid out in the binders. Strategy and execution are intertwined and to talk about one without understanding the other is both naive and, for many businesses, competitively disastrous.

Over the past two decades there have been several hundred books and thousands of articles written on strategy execution, strategy deployment, and a host of other names. Some have been written by highly experienced and successful CEOs, like the popular book *Execution: The Discipline of Getting Things Done* by Larry Bossidy and Ram Charan. Others are more academic such as *The Execution Premium* by Robert Kaplan and David Norton, and *Strategic Vision: Effective Corporate Action with Hoshin Planning* by Michael Cowley and Ellen Domb. And there is a plethora in between, such as *Real-Time Strategic Change* by Robert W. Jacobs or *Rapid Transformation* by Behnam Tabrizi.

Yes, I've read all these, and many more. But you don't have to. This book, **FASTBREAK: The CEO's Guide to Strategy Execution** is designed as a synthesis of the best wisdom out there combined with my own hands-on experience as a consultant on culture change, turnarounds and strategy execution. It is not intended to be an exhaustive treatise on the subject, but instead as a guide book, full of suggestions, landmarks, rarely revealed information, tips and insights you can use to navigate your way to significant improvement in your company's ability to deliver on its strategic and business objectives.

Whenever I go to a foreign country or major city, even one I've been to before, I always take with me one of the illustrated travel guides. The one with all the pictures and maps of little-known places to stay and interesting things to see. It helps bring the country or city to life so I am better able to enjoy my visits. Think of this short work as your guidebook to improved strategy execution.

In this book I am going to approach the subjects of strategy and execution in an integrated manner combing the elements of planning, alignment, focus, discipline, governance, culture and leadership. Strategy and execution go together.

"Stratecution" isn't really a word, but you get the picture.

Why Focus on the CEO?

Because it's the CEO who gets fired if the strategy doesn't get implemented!

There is no execution without leadership!

My first real awareness of this fact was in 1987 when, as a busy consultant travelling the globe I watched Richard Ferris, CEO of United Airlines, get sacked after his failed strategy of creating a *"one stop, integrated experience for travelers"* by combining United Airlines, Hertz Rent-a-Car and Westin Hotels into a new company, Allegis. It was a brilliant strategy, but the execution never happened and Ferris got the boot. There's a long list of CEOs ousted over the lack of ability to deliver on strategies they enthusiastically sold to investors and Boards.

In my experience, there are just four key requirements in the role of the CEO:

- Get the right people on the bus
- Craft a competitive strategy
- Get the best out of those people
- Execute, Execute, Execute

Strategy execution is a leadership issue, not a management issue. In most organizations the CEO is the only one with a truly horizontal, enterprise-wide view across the company, while everyone else is focused on their functional or business unit objectives. It's up to the CEO to get the strategy in place and drive the execution forward. If you think it's the job of the strategic planning department, pack your bags!

The good news is that most CEOs have a pretty clear vision for their organization. I suppose it is part of the DNA of a good CEO; they just know where the company needs to go, how to beat the competition, how to delight customers and how to grow the business. More often than not the analytics confirm their directional instincts.

The issue is not where to go, nor even how to get there, but actually getting everyone in the organization to do what needs to be done! I have had many long discussions with frustrated business leaders who cannot seem to get their organization aligned and delivering on the strategy. They often have a very clear plan, and most are highly articulate, giving presentation after presentation about the strategy and vision. Heads nod, commitments are made, but soon the momentum stalls. The next set of discussions I tend to have with the CEO is who to replace on the senior team because someone is obviously not getting the message.

Sometimes out of sheer frustration and to speed things up, the CEO will hire one of the big consulting firms to implement a cost savings project. *"If I can't get faster traction on the strategy, then at least I can get some cost out and buy myself some time."*

So for those CEOs who are willing to look at strategy and execution in an integrated way, this guide will be extremely useful. And it's not just for the CEO. Anyone in a leadership position who is tasked with executing plans against difficult odds will find practical tools and hope in this guidebook.

Why Me?

The Strategy-on-a-Page Execution Roadmap and the overall **FASTBREAK Strategy Execution** process described in this guidebook are the culmination of more than three decades of consulting assignments, across multiple industries, to improve business performance. Sometimes with stellar results and other times not even moving the dial. My colleagues and I have taken all our combined consulting experiences, analyzed the successes and failures, reviewed all the management skills and consulting tools used, and then asked a single question:

> *What is the simplest, most robust process for ensuring the successful execution of strategy?*

What we have developed is a philosophy and a methodology, along with a toolkit that can be used by any organization, of any size, at any stage of its development, to greatly ensure the successful delivery of strategic (and operational) business objectives.

My interest in strategy execution evolved slowly, and sometimes painfully. In 1978 I co-founded, along with Dr. Larry E. Senn, a consulting firm specializing in reshaping corporate culture and aligning senior executive teams: The Senn-Delaney Leadership Consulting Group. In those early days, the words corporate culture hadn't been popularized. Instead we talked about the *'personality of the organization'*, the analogy akin to the personality strengths and weaknesses of an individual and the habitual behaviors that seemed to follow.

Some people have open personalities, others more defensive and closed. Some have inquisitive, risk-taking personalities, others cynical and risk averse. Some are highly analytical and detailed; others seem to live by the seat of their pants. We discovered that organizations also had definable *'personalities'* and characteristic ways of behaving that impacted their ability to deliver results and most importantly, to implement necessary change.

Then in 1982 Tom Peters and Bill Waterman published their hugely popular book, *In Search of Excellence*, and suddenly everyone was talking about corporate culture. Well, our firm had first mover advantage and over the next 20 years we grew the firm and had the opportunity to work with many major US and global businesses. Again, working with the senior team to help them understand that *'organizations are shadows of their leaders'* (that's the good news and the bad news) and that culture change could, in many cases, be a key to improved business performance.

After over 20 years as President and CEO of the Senn-Delaney Leadership Consulting Group and several million frequent flyer miles, in 2000 I retired and took my family to live in the South of France for a couple of years. It was there that I had the time and the luxury to review the past several decades of consulting assignments and to figure out just exactly what I had learned.

I knew, beginning about 8 years before, that while we were doing great work on senior team alignment and culture change, something important was missing.

More often than not our consulting assignments led to a huge surge of enthusiasm and shifts in leadership attitudes and behavior, but we weren't dealing with the underlying business processes that, in my mind at least, could better sustain a business transformation.

My new quest became how to integrate culture change and leadership alignment with business process improvement in a way that leads to dramatic and sustainable business transformation. It has been an exciting period of learning and discovery.

Over the past 10 years we have developed the **FASTBREAK Strategy Execution** process and **Strategy-on-a-Page Execution Roadmap** and partnered with such major organizations as Ford of Europe, British Telecom, BSkyB, AxleTech International, General Dynamics Armament Systems, and numerous other companies to focus on turnaround and strategy execution

And just what is strategy?

I am going to break from the traditional understanding of strategy and present a new, more comprehensive and, I believe useful definition. In my view, strategy is no longer a series of binders full of charts and analyses that determine how the company will focus its resources over a long period of time. Real strategy is much more dynamic and cannot be divorced from execution.

Strategy is a contact sport! It's not just analytics, plans, market assessments, competitor analysis, PowerPoint presentations and growth charts. These are important but not sufficient.

One of the better experts on business strategy is Dr. Richard Rumelt, a professor at the UCLA Andersen School of Management. Rumelt pulls no punches in attacking most strategies as fluff or consultant gobbledygook (love that word) and instead presents a real world look at strategy. If you haven't read his most recent book, *Good Strategy, Bad Strategy*, the first few chapters are packed with practical wisdom about what strategy is and isn't.

This is how he defines strategy:

> *Strategy is a coherent set of analyses, concepts,*
> *policies, arguments and actions that respond to*
> *a high-stakes challenge. A strategy coordinates*
> *action to address a specific challenge.*

As you can see, Rumelt goes far beyond the bulging binders full of charts and graphs to include **ACTION**. And throughout his writing and teaching he stresses the critical role of leadership and making decisions in the overall strategy execution process. Many of us believe that strategy is as much about what not to do as it is about what to focus on. The key here is making choices and not trying to do everything or be excellent in all areas.

Another proponent of a realistic approach to strategy and execution is Professor Henry Mintzberg of McGill University. In his book *Strategy Bites Back*, (a highly academic book, yet written with a tongue-in-cheek style) he and his coauthors take the academic world of strategy to task. In a nutshell this great book implies, and proves, that *"strategy comes from human actions, but never from human plans."*

FASTBREAK: The CEO's Guide to Strategy Execution is built on the premise that strategy and execution are inseparable; distinct yet fused together. To separate the two sides of a coin is to destroy its functionality. The same is true of strategy and execution.

> *There is no strategy without execution, and there is no execution without leadership!*

To win at strategy execution, you and your leadership team need to be 100% committed and fully engaged. You must debate, argue, put forward alternative approaches, move around company assets, hold each other accountable, set shared objectives and focus more on moving the company forward than obsessing over departmental goals. And it can get 'hot' in these meetings, as it should. After all, nothing exciting ever happens in a refrigerator. It gets tense, loud and sometimes frustrating.

One CEO described it like this: *"We argue and debate. Nobody gets everything they want, yet everyone wins."*

Strategy execution is a form of rugby in pinstripes. Yet with the proper strategy execution process, and by adhering to a set of leadership principles, you can deliver a highly workable set of interlocking action plans and shared objectives, with clear team ground rules, focus and commitment. As a result, the senior team gets aligned, the company gets engaged and the strategy gets traction.

Health Warning

This is a good time for a word of caution. Your strategy execution journey won't be easy! Many books on strategy, leadership and organization performance give you formulas, the 21 irrefutable laws, examples and motivational stories in an attempt to convince the reader that if they just follow the plan (or implement the formula) everything will be rosy. After all, the purpose of a business self-help book is to motivate you, not depress you.

Well, let me go on record right here. Strategy execution is not easy, not for the faint-hearted, and in fact, never goes according to plan. Like making sausage, it can get ugly and chaotic, but the product or outcome is worth the effort. Even if you only improve your ability to effectively deliver your strategic objectives by 30-50%, that's a huge improvement to your bottom line, to customer satisfaction and in your competitive positioning. And, along the way, you and your leadership team will grow in capability, alignment and confidence.

So, if you are ready, fasten your seat belt, put on your crash helmet and let's get started!

Chapter 1:

EXECUTION IS THE COMPETITIVE ADVANTAGE

In May 1944, the Allies were in the final planning stages of Operation Overlord, the plan to invade Europe, commonly known as D-Day. Deceptions had been in place for some time, running counter-intelligence that left the Germans guessing the landing places and the size of the force. For the Allies, everything hinged on a knife-edge where even a vague weather forecast made for many sleepless nights. The Allied Senior Staff knew losses would be high in any attempted invasion. The Germans after all had years to plan their defense of the French coast, and only a few years earlier had planned their own invasion across the Channel. If the enemy guessed right, or unlucky weather interrupted the landing force, disaster loomed, not victory.

Put in terms of strategy, the intent was clear: to attempt the biggest amphibious landing in history, recapture France and invade Germany. It also had to be somewhat of a surprise as well. Reading the diaries of Field Marshal Lord Alanbrooke, the Chief of the General Staff of the UK Military Command, one is struck by the work ethic, the endless travel and almost inhuman pressures.

Alanbrooke toured his operations endlessly, talked to officers and observed the preparations first hand, evaluated new ideas and technology, made crucial "HR" decisions on commanders and assignments, dealt with the politics, and managed the egos of generals and statesman. But he never lost sight of the strategic intent: first to defend Britain, and then to defeat Germany.

As a case study in linking up strategy and execution, Operation Overlord had a strategic vision, breakthrough objectives, measured milestones and specific accountabilities all clearly linked up and committed to at the top. And they were focused on execution, not excuses. The top leaders moved swiftly to remove commanders that didn't deliver results. Everyone had to perform, period.

Fast forward to modern conflicts and here we find General David Petraeus cutting to the essence of strategy and focusing relentlessly on execution. When asked about alternative plans for the US strategy in Iraq, his response was crisp: *"There is a Plan B. Make Plan A. work."*

Two of my favorite spokesmen and authors on business issues are Jack Welch and Jim Collins. While different characters from different worlds – the corporate world and academia – both have great insight into business and organizational life, and especially the topic of strategy execution.

> *The important thing is not having a strategy,*
> *it's getting it implemented. ~ Jack Welch*

If you are a business executive reading this book and don't know who John F. (Jack) Welch Jr. is, you must have been living on another planet for the past 30 years. Business people either love or hate Jack Welch, but it's tough to deny his performance as a

Chief Executive. As CEO of General Electric from 1981-2001, Jack Welch increased the market value of GE from $14 billion to more than $410 billion at the time of his retirement, making it the most valuable and largest company in the world. In 1999, *Fortune Magazine* named him "Manager of the Century," and the *Financial Times* recently named him one of the three most admired business leaders in the world today. He's also very outspoken, on lots of subjects, but especially on strategy execution.

Much of the phenomenal growth of GE was achieved through the discipline of execution Welch instilled in his executives, those that lasted anyway. And numerous executives at General Electric trained by Welch went on to be very successful CEOs, including Larry Bossidy, Stanly Gault, Jim McNerney, David Johnston, Larry Cote, Jeffrey Immelt and Matt Espe, to name a few. All these executives took away similar valuable lessons from their GE experience; develop a simple plan, keep repeating it, and hold people accountable for delivery.

> *However you slice it, lack of management discipline*
> *correlates with poor implementation, and passionate*
> *adherence to management discipline leads to effective*
> *implementation. ~ Jim Collins, Good to Great*

Jim Collins, on the other hand, comes about his deep insights into business success and failure and the importance of execution through objective research, studying numerous companies over long periods of time, and digging into the factors that guide those few companies that continually stand out from their industry peers. Most of his books are international best sellers, including *Good to Great, Built to Last,* and *How the Mighty Fall.*

Collins began his research and teaching career on the faculty at Stanford Graduate School of Business, receiving the Distinguished Teaching Award in 1992. In 1995, he founded a management laboratory in Boulder, Colorado, where he conducts research and consults with executives from around the world. He is even on the faculty of West Point where he teaches leadership.

Different lives, different paths, similar points of view: **execution matters, big time**.

If you are a CEO reading this, here's my point. Focused and disciplined execution can be your single biggest competitive advantage! But it will take four things from you: a clear plan, a robust execution process, courage, and your 100% commitment to hold people accountable.

> *Execution is a specific set of behaviors and techniques*
> *that companies need to master in order to have*
> *competitive advantage. It is a discipline of its own.*
> *~ Larry Bossidy and Ram Charan*

Chapter 2:
THE OPPORTUNITY

I love it when a plan comes together!
~ John 'Hannibal' Smith, the A-Team TV Series

Most business books begin by describing the problem and then grow it to the size of Mt. Everest with statistics, charts and horror stories of company failures and incompetent leadership decisions. No wonder the genre of business fable (*Who Stole My Cheese, Our Iceberg is Melting, Death by Meeting,* and others) is so popular. They are entertaining, even motivating, easy to read, and of course they contain nuggets of insight along the way.

Taking a different approach, I'm going to start this book not with the problem, but with the opportunity. The good news. The pot of gold at the end of the rainbow. In this day and age of global financial upheaval, new competition from every corner and rapidly changing business models, it's easy to feel overwhelmed. A natural tendency is to hunker down, cut costs, ride out the storm and hope to survive until the next economic upturn.

Hope is not a strategy! ~ Michael Bloomberg

The opportunity today, right now, amidst all the current chaos, is huge. And execution is your competitive advantage. Those who deliver on their strategic objectives, while everyone else is tiptoeing around in default mode, can rapidly put distance between themselves and the competition, capture significant market share and build customer loyalty.

Consider Zappos. In 1999, would you have invested money in an on-line, Internet shoe retailer? Especially in an industry where everyone knows how important it is to physically try on the product, see how it looks and feels, and be helped by a knowledgeable experienced shoe salesman. Besides, the Internet and Internet retailing was still in its infancy and very few people were comfortable giving up their credit card details over the phone, let alone on the Internet. Not many gave Zappos a snowball's chance in hell (maybe that's why they are headquartered in Las Vegas).

But to Tony Hsieh, the guiding force and CEO of Zappos, the strategy was simple: build a strong corporate culture and deliver excellent customer service. The definitive task would be execution: how to actually sell lots of different brands of shoes directly to customers through the Internet while giving world-class customer service.

While Tony and the team believed with all their body and soul that corporate culture needed to be the foundation of the company, they also knew they needed robust business processes that were in alignment with their unique culture in order to deliver consistent, world-class customer service. With these two principles in place, Zappos, headquartered in remote Henderson, Nevada (outside of Las Vegas) went from $0 in 1999 to $1 billion in revenue in 2009, at which time they were bought by Amazon. That's right zero to $1 billion in 10 years!

Recently Zappos published a book about their culture. What I find interesting is that the culture doesn't just come from a strict hiring profile. It comes from a myriad of imbedded business processes (outsiders would call them people processes) that help perpetuate the unique Zappos service culture. Culture in alignment with robust business processes designed to fit the business strategy are a potent combination. A strong culture with poor processes leads to service breakdowns, just as strong business processes and a weak, or negative, culture leads to inconsistent performance on all fronts.

So, here's an example of the available opportunity. Zero to $1 billion in 10 years through a combination of processes focusing on culture and supply chain. If they can deliver consistent business performance and outdistance the competition, why can't your company?

From Worst to First!

Success has no autopilot switch. ~ Gordon Bethune

Here's an example of opportunity in a lousy industry: the turnaround of Continental Airlines between 1994 and 1996. It may be a slightly dated example, but it clearly illustrates the principles behind effective strategy execution. For one of the most interesting and entertaining reads about business and leadership, I suggest you pick up the book *From Worst to First*, by former Continental CEO, Gordon Bethune. Believe it or not, it's a page-turner and as a CEO you will painfully recognize many of the issues he describes as they went to work on the turnaround.

I'll give you a brief overview. Here's the situation at Continental

Airlines in 1994:

- Company facing its third bankruptcy in a decade
- $2.5 bn in default; not debt, default
- 10 years of consecutive losses
- Amalgamation of 7 airlines, and very different cultures, with 40,000 employees
- Worst record among the 10 US airlines: dead last in
  - Baggage complaints
  - On-time departures and arrivals
  - Involuntary denied boarding
- 10 CEOs in 10 years

Want to sign up for that job? Gordon Bethune, an executive from Boeing and a former mechanic and pilot, thought the Board of Continental was nuts when they offered him the job. But Gordon knew that the issue wasn't lack of money; they had raised money twice before and their performance hadn't improved. The issue was lack of focus, leadership, a simple plan people could believe in, and a robust execution process.

> *Anytime you are in a company that is broken, often what has been ignored are three things: the people, the training of those people, and the systems. ~ Lawrence Kellner, CFO Continental Airlines*

Here's the situation in 1996, just two years later:

- Continental Airlines returned to profitability in 1995
- 1996: Voted airline of the year, against 300 global competitors
- Ranked in the top 5 of all global airlines ever since 1996
- Among the top 4 in all DOT airline service statistics since 1996
- 16 straight quarters of record profits
- Share price from $3.30 to $50 in 4 years

- Employee turnover reduced 45%

Gordon and the senior team at Continental created outstanding results using a clear and focused strategy execution process, coupled with strong and committed leadership.

How do you want your mattress, madam?

Everyday day I come to work energized for two simple reasons. One, I love our product. Two, I love helping people improve their lives. ~Bill McLaughlin, CEO of Select Comfort

What could be a more lackluster and uninspiring industry than the manufacturing and selling of mattresses? Especially when a new bed is purchased by a customer once every 10 years, or longer. How do you turnaround a $250 million mattress company losing $2-3 million a month?

Select Comfort, a retailer of adjustable-firmness mattresses, was founded in 1987 by an inventor and former innerspring mattress maker who wanted a better night's sleep. While the sleep experience was great, the fortunes of the company weren't so positive. Growing fast throughout the early and mid-1990s, it wound up in late 1999 with expensive costs, high overheads, disjointed diversification programs, and losing $26 million.

That's when Bill McLaughlin, former CEO of Frito-Lay Europe became the fourth Select Comfort CEO in 12 months [7] [8]

Bill was the right CEO for us three years ago. He's the right CEO today. And he'll be the right CEO five to seven years from now. ~ Pat Hopf, Chairman, Select Comfort

That was 2001. Fast forward three years later and Select Comfort is a $460M company whose share price has risen from $0.45 to $31.00. And today? Select Comfort operates 400+ retail stores in the US, Canada and Australia, and has revenues of over $900 million.

So what did Bill do that others didn't? One of the first things Bill realized was the tremendous pride about the mission and purpose of the company and the importance of its products.

> *Basically, this company was founded on a strong belief that people's health depended upon a good night's sleep. It wasn't just a marketing slogan, it was a religion to the employees, says McLaughlin.*

The turnaround at Select Comfort is a case study in leadership, focus and strategy execution. Leadership, as practiced by Bill McLaughlin, is getting people to do what needs to be done, having a robust execution process, and having fun doing it. Bill is a people person and a great believer in training and listening to people. But at the same time he is keen on developing sound strategies and robust business processes.

Just recently (June 2012), Bill passed the title of CEO to an insider, Shelly Ibach, who continues the tradition of superior strategy execution, recently posting strong sales and a share increase of 19% at the end of the 2nd Quarter, 2012.

So What?

These are just three stories out of many where strong, committed leadership combined with an effective strategy execution process created significant and lasting results. These stories are meant to encourage you to read on, to see what is possible in your business with the understanding and use of the principles and tools in *FASTBREAK: The CEO's Guide to Strategy Execution.*

Chapter 3:
THE CEO'S LAMENT: EXECUTION, EXECUTION, EXECUTION

Life is what happens while you are busy making other plans. ~ John Lennon

Competition is what happens while you are busy making strategic plans.

All businesses require a *'strategy'*. In essence, a strategy is a defined set of actions to achieve success against competition. To be effective, the strategy needs to be forward thinking, based on deep insights into opportunities and capabilities, and a product of clear thinking, honest assessments and effective decision-making. But most importantly, to be effective the strategy must be executed in a way that achieves the desired results.

Unfortunately, the statistics on effective strategy execution are universally dismal. The fact is most companies have a poor track record of strategy execution:

- A 2004 survey of 276 senior operating executives by *The Economist* found that 57% of the companies had been unsuccessful in executing on strategic initiatives over the previous three years. [9]

- In a 2006 survey of more than 1,500 executives by the American Management Association and the Human Resource Institute, only 3% of respondents rated their companies as very successful at executing corporate strategies, while 62% described their organizations as mediocre or worse [10]

- In a recent survey of 200 FTSE 1000 companies, 80% of directors said they had the right strategy, but only 14% thought they were implementing well. [11]

- A survey of 400 companies found that 49% of the leaders reported a gap between their organization's ability to formulate a strategy and its ability to deliver results. Shockingly, only 36% of leaders who thought their company had an execution gap expressed confidence in their organization's ability to close the gap. [12]

- In a recent McKinsey Quarterly survey of 2,207 executives, only 28% said that the quality of strategic decisions in their companies was generally good, 60% thought that bad decisions were about as frequent as good ones, and the remaining 12% thought good decisions were altogether infrequent. [13]

- In a recent McKinsey & Co study of 197 companies, despite 97% of directors believing they had the right 'strategic vision', only 33% reported achieving 'significant strategic success'. [14]

- 70% of CEOs who get fired do so not because of bad strategy, but because of poor execution. [1]

Our experience and research shows numerous, often interconnected reasons why strategy deployment and change initiatives are difficult to deliver:

- Execution is usually an afterthought rather than an integral part of strategy formulation

- Lack of clearly defined accountability for strategic initiatives and overall objectives

- Poor alignment at the top and heavy 'silo focus' leads to sub-optimization and resource conflicts, wasting valuable management time

- Many initiatives are not directly linked to key strategic objectives. Too often we see 'pet' projects buried inside the overall strategy, thus wasting resources on 'Disconnected Initiatives.'

- Less than 14% of employees have seen or understand the strategy. [15] Without understanding the company strategy, employee engagement and new ideas for improvement are limited.

- Corporate culture often acts as a barrier to the teamwork, openness and innovation required for effective strategy delivery.

- Disciplined governance of strategic initiatives is notoriously lacking and 'day to day' operations problems often hijack the attention of the senior team away from strategic issues. Recent studies have shown that less than 5% of the senior team's time is spent on strategic issues. [16]

- Too often the strategy is developed by an outside consulting firm (after interviewing executives, of course), delivered to management in a dazzling presentation and a thick deck of slides, but with little real 'ownership' by those left behind to implement it. Commitment is lacking from the beginning and only diminishes as difficulties are encountered.

These and other barriers often combine to create the perfect storm, where an otherwise good strategy winds up being abandoned as *'too difficult'* or *'not right for us'*, or in many cases, business-as-usual objectives get substituted for strategic objectives. As a result the company makes incremental progress when it really requires breakthrough performance.

Management Fatigue

Fatigue makes cowards of us all. ~Vince Lombardi

Two great sports coaches with unprecedented winning records, Vince Lombardi and John Wooden, both believed that fitness and conditioning were the secret weapons of winning teams and each made fitness a part of every practice and the daily regimen of their teams. With fitness comes the mental and physical stamina to execute well and quickly turn an opponent's mistake into a score.

Over the past several years I've noticed a definite trend occurring in business – management fatigue. Managers are bone-tired and feeling frazzled. And as a result I see good managers making silly mistakes, not always thinking clearly, short-tempered with their peers and staff, less creative and allowing negativity and cynicism to creep in.

One of the reasons they are fatigued is lack of exercise and a general deteriorating level of personal fitness. Most of us in the management and business ranks are overweight and out of shape. And it's getting to be an epidemic the world over. Fast foods, poor diets, skipping meals, alcohol and lack of exercise all contribute to management fatigue.

I'm tired, the kind of tired you can't sleep off.
~ Frank Reagan, NYC Police Commissioner in TV Series
Blue Bloods

But there is another, more insidious type of management fatigue and it's harder to cure. It attacks the mind and some believe even erodes the soul. This management fatigue shows up as an overall lack of enthusiasm for the work. Mental management fatigue is the result of the frustrations of trying to make things happen inside organizations with poor business processes.

Every time we try to improve something around here it
feels like we are pushing on a rope.

For example, there is a growing resistance (and resentment) against meetings. The fact is, most meetings are poorly run, longer than necessary, reach few decisions, and are fraught with hidden agendas, interpersonal conflicts and lack of candor and teamwork. Several managers have described their meetings as trying to sprint through Molasses (Treacle for my UK friends). Lots of energy is expended (and hot air as well) with little results. After months or years of putting up with bad meetings and trying to get something accomplished, managers just get mentally tired of it all. Then the door is open for cynicism and negativity. In some organizations, the culture can be described as cynicism fueled by chronic management fatigue.

Meetings are indispensable
when you don't want to do anything.
~ John Kenneth Galbraith

Another major contributor to mental management fatigue is the strategy execution process, or in reality in most companies, the non-process. As a result of not having a robust, enterprise-wide strategy execution process, many execution issues get bogged down in turf wars where executives are bickering over limited resources instead of swiftly moving the strategy forward. Meetings tend to drag on with little hope of real decisions or sustainable solutions. And what's insidious about meetings and strategy execution is that they are daily events. There is rarely a holiday from meetings and moving the strategy forward takes continuous attention. These issues are with managers every day. So frustration and management fatigue build up, slowing down the momentum ever more.

Chapter 4:
SLEEPING POLICEMEN AND OTHER BARRIERS
TO STRATEGY EXECUTION

*However beautiful the strategy, you should occasionally
look at the results! ~ Winston Churchill*

In England they call them *'sleeping policemen.'* The French term is
'dos d'ane' which translates to donkey's back. Similarly in Spanish
they are called *'lomo de burro'*. Speed bumps are used the world
over as a means of slowing traffic, especially through populated
areas. On the Galapagos Island of Santa Cruz, there is a road
through a national forest that is home to several rare species of
Galapagos Finches (small birds which have adapted to various
ecological niches). It seems that large trucks hauling goods went so
fast along this small stretch that numerous finches were killed as
they flew from one side of the road to the other. With speed
bumps in place the rare finch population is now protected.

Some neighborhoods with lots of children have even erected their own as a safety precaution. There are even *'dynamic'* speed bumps that deflate if you are going at or below the proper speed, and for emergency vehicles as well (the wonders of technology).

Have you ever been in a hurry to get somewhere in your car and suddenly hit a speed bump that you didn't see? Not only does it jar your teeth, but it also rattles your car and increases the wear and tear on your automobile. Hit enough speed bumps going too fast and your car will be due for a visit to the auto repair shop, while you are at the dentist getting loose fillings repaired.

It's the same with strategy execution. The road ahead is littered with speed bumps that not only slow down forward momentum, but can also derail you from reaching your strategic and business objectives. What is really weird is how some organizations seem to back up and go over them again and again while other teams turn speed bumps into launching ramps!

In Chapter Two I listed numerous barriers to effective strategy execution:

- Deployment is usually an afterthought rather than an integral part of strategy formulation
- Lack of clearly defined accountability for strategic initiatives and overall objectives
- Less than 14% of employees have seen or understand the strategy [15]
- Corporate culture often acts as a barrier to the levels of teamwork, openness and innovation required for effective strategy delivery.
- Disciplined governance of strategic initiatives is notoriously lacking and 'day to day' operations problems often hijack the attention of the senior team away from longer term issues. Recent studies have shown that less than 5% of the senior team's time is spent on strategic issues. [16]
- Too often the strategy is developed by an outside

consulting firm (after interviewing executives, of course), delivered to management in a dazzling presentation and a thick deck of slides, but with little real 'ownership' by those left behind to implement it. Commitment is lacking from the beginning and only diminishes as difficulties are encountered.

- Poor alignment at the top and heavy 'silo' focus leads to sub-optimization and resource conflicts, wasting valuable management time.

- Many initiatives are not directly linked to key strategic objectives. Too often we see 'pet' projects buried inside the overall strategy, thus wasting resources on 'disconnected initiatives.'

Let's explore these in more detail. I believe very few CEOs and executives are aware of these speed bumps and how they negatively impact strategy execution.

Execution as an 'Afterthought'

We will not have peace by afterthought
.~ Norman Cousins

One of the breakthroughs in modern manufacturing was the development of a process called Design for Manufacturability (DFM). Previously, product design and manufacturing tended to operate as isolated groups. The designers would come up with a 'cool' design, do their market research and customer focus groups and decide on the best design for a given product. Then they would send their designs to manufacturing for production, having done their job.

In most cases, however, manufacturing had difficulty building the product to the exact design specs, often due to material constraints and production process difficulties. And once the product was produced, the cost was often greater than the market would bear. Then the bickering between design and manufacturing began, each pointing the finger at the other for why the product didn't sell well.

The solution is simple and is an example of breakthrough thinking. Get designers and manufacturing people to work together during the early design phases so that this *'cool'* design can be easily manufactured. Each group shares its knowledge and expertise with the other and jointly work together. And one of the basic principles of DFM is the KIS principle: *'Keep it Simple'*. The fewer number of parts, and the ability to use standard parts, keeps down costs and speeds up the manufacturing process.

Unfortunately there is not much DFE (Design for Executability) in the deployment of strategy. Execution is typically an afterthought! The strategy task force has done its work, produced a 100-page document with 65 PowerPoint slides, disbanded and gone back to their day jobs. The strategy may be perfect, but did anyone ask if the company has the management or leadership capabilities to actually deliver the strategy? Do we have the resources and skill sets required? Do we have access to required funding? Do we have the kind of culture that can change in the ways required to deliver on the strategy? The plan is good, but executability is definitely missing. Good luck on delivering your strategy.

It's Not My Job!

If everyone is accountable, no one is accountable!

Lack of clearly defined accountability for strategic initiatives and objectives is one of the more insidious speed bumps. I have read literally hundreds of strategy documents and I can list on one hand those that actually have specified owners by name assigned for the delivery of objectives and initiatives. In most cases, the initiatives are distributed to the *'appropriate functions'* (people stuff to HR, product stuff to Engineering, sales initiatives to Business Development, etc.), who in turn set up a variety of ad-hoc functional teams to progress the initiatives, while holding down their day jobs as well.

While a senior executive usually becomes the 'sponsor' or 'champion' for the initiative, finding one person who is definitely accountable, who accepts total ownership for the delivery and success of that particular strategic initiative is like trying to find the person who farted in the elevator. The smell is there but nobody takes ownership. And in my mind one of the most wasted titles (and wastes of time) in business is the executive 'sponsor' or 'champion'; and much of that time is wasted in briefing meetings. Nothing gets decided or improved, just another briefing so the 'sponsor' is in the know. Ask any program manager or initiative owner the value of these briefing meetings, and then cover your ears!

The Great 'Untapped'

One of my favorite TV shows is *Star Trek.* Now I did watch the original *Star Trek* with Captain Kirk, Mr. Spock and Doctor McCoy almost religiously and loved every episode. But it went off the air and I went to graduate school and it was 18 years before a new version hit television. *Star Trek: The Next Generation* episodes were less macho and portrayed leadership as more (dare I say) 'sensitive', more collegial and less 'all knowing.' Captain Picard was the modern leader.

But what really hooked me on the new series was the 'Holodeck'; a large room on the Enterprise where the computer could create any reality as a hologram environment such that the crew could live out their fantasies. They could have the computer create a program to simulate the wild west of the early 19th century and pretend to be small town Marshalls and outlaws, or create the illusion of sailing on a pirate ship. Great fun.

Now the concept of a hologram is pretty interesting. I can't fathom the math or the physics, but one way to describe a hologram is to compare it to a photograph. If you take a photograph and cut it in half you get a left piece and a right piece, which, when put together, make the picture whole. Cutting the photograph into 4 pieces would give you four different parts of the original photo.

A hologram is a very different kind of picture. If you (could) cut a holographic picture in half, each half would contain the entire original picture. Cutting it into quarters would give four complete original pictures, only smaller. And so on. You could cut the hologram into a hundred pieces and each piece would be a complete version of the original picture, just smaller.

In my view, your strategy should be more like a holographic picture and less like a traditional photograph. No matter whom you talk with in the company, they should have a complete understanding of the overall strategy. Yes, they may focus their efforts on a certain segment of the strategy that pertains to their role or expertise, but they also understand that the strategy is not just a series of individual actions, but an integrated set of activities that all work together to deliver the end result.

That's not the case, however, in most organizations. Very few employees have any understanding at all of the company strategy. At most, they have one of the torn sections of the photo, a piece of information about the whole, but not the whole.

It seems to me that if innovation, efficiency and cost savings are critical for business sustainability in today's constrained global economy, then getting employees, especially those closest to the customer, to better understand the company strategy and business objectives would be an asset. Without an understanding of the company strategy, how do we expect to fire up employee engagement and generate new ideas for improvement? Yet the fact remains that many employees, if not most, only know their narrow job goals or objectives. Not very inspiring when day after day all you are responsible for are narrow goals such as sales calls per hour or number of customer calls-answered within three rings!

There are several reasons why strategy and big picture goals are not well understood among employees. The first reason seems to be the belief (erroneous I would say) that employees don't care about lofty company visions or strategies and only care about their own work, a paycheck and advancement. This, I believe, is an outdated belief carried forward from Victorian times and still held by those with elitist management views. Somehow they have the view that employees are less committed than management and not inherently interested in ideas or making things better.

Yet these same employees, who seem to have checked their brains at the door every morning, manage large budgets for their churches, volunteer to help build community centers, run e-commerce websites from their homes, restore vintage WW2 aircraft, rebuild racing cars, and a myriad of other highly complex endeavors. Why? Because they like the challenge and the opportunity to make a difference. Yet at work they are not engaged!

The human brain is a wondrous instrument. It starts working the moment you wake up and doesn't stop until you get to the office. ~ Robert Frost

Because of this old-fashioned belief, management looks at the cost of strategy communications workshops, and quarterly all-hands meetings (where it is possible to engage in real dialogue and interact with employees about real business issues) and instead decide on a newsletter!

Another reason so few employees understand the overall

company strategy and vision is that up until now there has been no efficient and effective way to communicate the strategy to hundreds (or thousands) of employees spread over the globe. The cost of travel and executive time is a big hurdle in these times of tight budgets.

I said *"up until now"*. The format for effective strategy execution detailed in this guide, the **Strategy-on-a-Page Execution Roadmap** is literally a *'plan on a page'* and not only guides the executive team in the discipline and governance of effective strategy delivery, but also is an outstanding tool for employee communication and engagement around the business strategies.

Blame it on the 'culture'

Corporate culture often acts as a barrier to the levels of teamwork, openness and innovation required for effective strategy delivery. In many companies, culture is the most invisible of all the speed bumps!

Corporate culture has a tremendous impact on a firm's ability to execute on its strategic objectives. Most strategies deal with ways of beating the competition and growing market share, revenues and profits. The usual approaches are new products, improved quality and speed to market, or rapid expansion to capture first-mover advantage. In all cases, the corporate culture can either act as a propellant, or an anchor.

After decades of studying and working on reshaping corporate culture, I tend to take a very pragmatic view of just what culture is. I see culture as the *'personality of an organization'* or more simply *'how we do things around here'*. As some people have introverted personalities and others are extroverts, and each individual's personality results in characteristic behaviors. The same is true for corporate culture.

And corporate culture is more than just the collection of everyday employee behaviors. A more comprehensive understanding of corporate culture takes into account, not only behaviors (mindset or personality), but also skills and business processes.

CEOs and senior executives we have worked with find the following definition easy to understand and use:

> *Corporate Culture is a combination of behaviors and business processes (formal and informal) that over time becomes the habitual approach employees use in solving business problems and interacting with each other.*

It is now well documented that corporate culture impacts the ability of a company to execute on its strategy and that a culture can either propel or hinder strategic and business agendas. [17]

The relationship between culture and strategy execution is easier to see with the understanding that Strategy – Structure – Culture are interlinked and for top performance, these three critical business elements must be in alignment.

In simple terms, everyone knows where we are going (strategy), it's clear who does what in the organization (structure), and we all understand the ground rules for working together and for getting things done (culture).

In less turbulent times when the pace of change was slower, organizations were able to gain alignment between these three critical elements and as a result produced efficient performance and long-term growth. However, with the explosion of technology, rapid globalization, aggressive new competition and shifting regulation, companies are often forced to develop and implement new strategies. And there is often the need to reorganize in order to line up the organization to match the new strategy.

The problem is, that's as far as most senior teams take it; thinking that improved performance should naturally follow. Because most CEOs and senior executives are often insulated from the real internal culture(s) within their organization, it becomes difficult to see the link between culture and performance. It also becomes

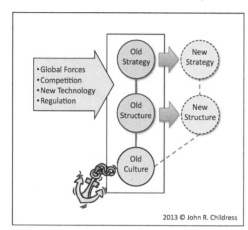

•Global Forces
•Competition
•New Technology
•Regulation

Old Strategy → New Strategy

Old Structure → New Structure

Old Culture

2013 © John R. Childress

difficult to see when the existing culture is no longer aligned with the new demands of the business.

Unless there is work done to reshape corporate culture, the old culture can act as an anchor, slowing down, and in some cases even stopping effective strategy execution. Therefore, to fully implement a new strategy or to rebuild your organization to be effective in a changed world, it is critical to reshape culture as well.

> *If you spend as much time on corporate culture*
> *as you do on the balance sheet, you will run a*
> *very successful organization.*

Who 'hijacked' our strategy?

> *If you had to identify, in one word, the reason*
> *why the human race has not achieved, and never*
> *will achieve, its full potential, that word would be*
> *'meetings' ~ Dave Barry*

Everywhere I go I hear complaints about Strategy Review Meetings. Whether they are held monthly, quarterly or on some other cadence, the comments from participants tend to be the same.

- *What a waste of time.*
- *Now I've lost another day of work.*
- *I flew to the East Coast for this? At least they had a decent movie on the flight.*
- *My team prepared for three days and they cut our time short.*
- *Lots of talk but no decisions, just another request for more data.*
- *I'm not really interested in what problems the other Directors have; I've got my own problems.*
- *The same three guys take up all the airtime. Like a broken record every meeting.*

The average strategy review meeting is anything but focused on strategy. It may have the intention of strategy review, but that's not what actually happens. What starts out as a review of the strategy quickly morphs into problem solving and fire-fighting on day-to-day operating problems. The three or four hours set aside for strategy turns into a full-court press on the current burning platform – a screaming customer, rejected shipments due to poor quality, ideas to make up this month's EBITDA shortfall. The list grows, but strategy is not on it.

Studies have shown that less than 5% of the senior team's time together is actually spent on strategic issues [16], the rest being hijacked by pressing day-to-day problems. It's no wonder much of the strategy has been forgotten (who was working on that?) and little progress has been made.

Co-mingling operational discussions with strategy review doesn't work. Period. What is missing in the strategy execution equation is a well-defined, purpose-built strategy review and governance process.

A while back I sat in the corporate office of Lewis Booth who, at the time, was CFO of Ford Motor Company. Lewis, along with the senior executive team led the successful turnaround and global repositioning of Ford.

Ford was the only one of the Big Three US automakers to refuse government bailout money, so they needed to be efficient and effective in everything they did to save the company. And their weekly (yes, you heard me right, weekly) 3 hour senior executive business and strategy review meetings are not only efficient and effective, but productive and strangely motivating as well. It has become such a major event within Ford that they often have visitors attend the meetings to see the process in action.

One of the reasons for the effectiveness of these meetings is the discipline instilled in the group as a result of good leadership from Alan Mulally, CEO. In addition, a standard set agenda, clear and inviolate ground rules, and standard templates make these weekly meetings highly effective.

Here are some of the ground rules the Ford senior team follows:

- Identify the problem, don't try to solve it during the meeting
- If you can help someone else solve a problem, talk to them after the meeting, not in the meeting
- Absolutely no '*pot shots*' or 'poking fun' at anyone, inside the room or out. Alan Mulally is very serious about this ground rule, as he understands deeply that respect for the individual and trust are the foundations of an effective team.
- Start each meeting with a review of the vision and mission (One Team – One Plan – One Goal)
- The Ford senior team has a list of 'expected behaviors' (how we agree to behave and lead) and these are reviewed at the start of every meeting

- Public appreciation was a part of many of these meetings (someone won an award or recognition, a 25-year service anniversary, etc.). In the words of Lewis Booth: *"We celebrated together when we had something to celebrate."*
- Everyone attends, either in person or via WebEx. I have a client where one of the senior team members refuses to travel to another location for their quarterly meetings – think about the hidden agenda and lack of alignment in that team.
- They go through nearly 300 slides in just over 2 hours as they review the entire business, but the trick is a common format and all new information is in blue, so they only need to focus on the blue material, not go over each slide in detail
- Each global region gets 10 minutes to present their charts and each *'Skill Center'* gets 5 minutes. They truly are efficient!
- They then use the exact same slides for their next level reviews, so everyone in management knows the same basic information in the same format.

Transparency of information, a commitment to solve problems as a team and help each other, and the fact that bonuses are based on how the company performs (not how their individual operations perform) help keep the Ford senior team highly focused and effective.

> *If everyone is moving forward together,*
> *then success takes care of itself.* ~ Henry Ford

The 'McKinsey' Gambit

Nobody ever got fired for hiring McKinsey!

One of the most critical ingredients in building a successful organization is to have a clear strategic agenda, which helps the company focus its energy and resources to create competitive advantage and also gives guidance on the number and scope of internal projects and initiatives that must be funded and resourced.

There are two schools of thought as to how to develop your strategic agenda. The most widely supported is to hire one of the top strategy consulting firms who come in and work with management to develop the strategic agenda. After all, they have the time, the manpower, the brains and certainly the experience to help you build a winning strategy and go forward agenda.

While this is the *'safest'* approach (no one ever got fired for hiring McKinsey), it has several drawbacks. First is the fact that, as these top-tier strategy firms have grown into global powerhouses, the quality of their work and advice has suffered. We all know of at least one CEO who received a '*boilerplate'* strategy, and some even had the previous client's name on it.

Okay, let's say you do get a strategy that was crafted just for you. The next drawback is the cost: normally several million. Okay, you can afford it and the Board is supportive. The real problem with outside firms helping you develop your strategy is the fact that in most cases they really don't help, they do all the work. It goes like this: an army of junior consultants descends upon your organization, gathers information, crunches numbers, holds focus groups, and work long into the night. The result is you may get a good (even great) strategy, but your management team doesn't really '*own'* it.

What we mean by lack of ownership is your team didn't do the hard thinking, sweat out the details and metrics, nor did they have the debates and arguments that result in a jointly agreed plan that everyone is committed to delivering. In most cases the plan was developed by an army of smart MBAs under the guidance of a senior consulting partner and delivered to your management team as an impressive PowerPoint presentation along with a stack of binders. I will wager a large amount that very few members of your senior team have read the entire strategy document, front to back! It's just not theirs! They aren't viscerally engaged, they aren't really excited about it, and this is one of the key reasons why good strategies fail to get delivered.

> *The difference between involvement and commitment*
> *is like ham and eggs at breakfast.*
> *The chicken is involved; the pig is committed.*

My point of view about developing a strategic agenda is to build it yourself: the CEO, the senior team and whoever else in the company has the capability and desire to contribute to building the future of the company.

I can hear the push-back already: *"We've got a business to run, we don't have the time, we've got a strategic planning department – it's their job. We're too close to the issue and need a broader, more global perspective."* The rationale goes on and on.

I take the opposite view: who knows your company, its capabilities, its strengths, its weaknesses, its customers better than you, not the leadership team and employees? And when the senior team and others take the time to have the debates, present and defend new initiatives, align around a strategy and breakthrough objectives, a curious thing happens. They *'own'* the plan. They created it. They understand it. It is theirs! And commitment is what you don't get when outsiders build the plan.

Okay, you might be saying, but where do we start? And how do we do it efficiently? In Chapter 8 we will be introducing you to a robust strategy development and execution process, the **Strategy-on-a-Page Execution Roadmap**, implemented by you and your leadership team that will significantly improve the probability of delivering your strategic objectives.

There is no strategy without execution,
and there is no execution without leadership!

The Two Major 'Speed Bumps'

There are two additional strategy execution speed bumps that can significantly derail the effective delivery of an otherwise good strategy. These are:

- **Disconnected Initiatives**: Many initiatives are not directly linked to key strategic objectives. Too often we see 'pet' projects buried inside the overall strategy, thus wasting resources on 'disconnected' initiatives.
- **Silo-Focus:** Poor alignment at the top and heavy 'silo' focus leads to sub-optimization and resource conflicts, wasting valuable management time and derailing strategy.

These are such powerful roadblocks that I have devoted the next two chapters to them.

Chapter 5:

DISCONNECTED INITIATIVES AND PROJECT OVERLOAD

The successful warrior is the average man, with laser-like focus. ~ Bruce Lee

The late Sir Peter Blake was a New Zealand yachtsman who won the Whitbread Round the World Race, the Jules Verne Trophy – setting the fastest time around the world of 74 days, 22 hours, 17 minutes, 22 seconds – and led Team New Zealand to successive victories in the America's Cup in 1995 and 2000. While the American teams had more money, New Zealand had a singularly effective strategy, the brainchild of Peter Blake [18].

When Blake was asked to take over as skipper for Team New Zealand, they weren't considered much of a contender, especially against the better-financed American *'Stars and Stripes'* boat. As you can imagine, there are a myriad of things that go into preparing a racing yacht for competition, from types of sails, ropes, winches and cranks, electronics, rigging, crew composition and training, and hundreds more. So with all these enablers and influencers for success, what should the team focus on? If you say all of them, then you have lost both time and money. Some are obviously more critical than others, yet all are required for success. Like any complicated endeavor, finding and keeping focus on the right things is crucial.

Peter Blake was a practical New Zealander and a veteran of ocean sailing and racing so instead of fancy spreadsheets and performance metrics, he focused the team on one single strategy: Will it make the boat go faster?

Every decision was evaluated against that one simple, yet holistic and powerful statement. The team began to rethink everything they knew about sailing and racing with this one strategic objective in mind. Training and team composition changed, equipment size and weight changed, sails changed. Even the crew comforts were looked at through the eyes of *'will it make the boat go faster'?* The result? Team spirit, alignment, focus, and back-to-back wins in 1995 and 2000.

> *What's the single yardstick your organization*
> *uses to determine how to allocate its scarce*
> *resources of time, people and money?*

Over the years I have worked with many organizations and senior teams as they struggle to implement their strategies and one of the key observations is the fact that organizations often have too many 'critical' objectives and corresponding initiatives. Not only do all these objectives compete for limited funding, but some even compete with each other.

Project Overload is also one of the major causes of cost inflation, reduced profitability, management stress, and poor morale. In fact, project overload is also one of the major reasons most strategies fail. It's not that the initiatives are not useful, but in most cases they are not directly linked to the overall strategic intent. As a result time, money and resources are spent on projects that don't specifically drive forward the company's strategic agenda.

I use a simple visual to display the situation and during speeches and executive workshops, more often than not, someone in the audience will remark: "that's our organization chart!"

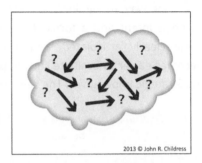

2013 © John R. Childress

Disconnected initiatives exist due to the fact that many of them are 'legacy' projects, left over from a previous leadership regime and strategic plan, or were acquired along with an acquisition and just left to carry on since management didn't want to disenfranchise the newly acquired managers. Many of these disconnected initiatives are well below the radar screen of senior management and often get buried inside a line item on departmental budgets and year after year they continue to be funded.

Searching out and killing those elusive disconnected initiatives is like trying to rid your lawn of crabgrass, or eliminating bamboo from the backyard fence. Finding them is not always easy and when you do, branding them as unessential creates an uproar from the sponsors of those projects deemed 'not connected':

- *"Are you trying to run my department or something?*
- *I'm paid to deliver my budget, which I do every year, so don't tell me what projects I can and cannot authorize.*
- *I wouldn't be funding them if I didn't think they weren't critical!"*

As a result, nobody looks forward to sorting out this mess and either they are allowed to continue or the CEO winds up playing Solomon with the baby.

The best way to diminish project overload is to have a clear strategic intent and a focused set of strategic imperatives. With these clearly articulated, and a clear execution roadmap, it becomes easier to evaluate current projects and initiatives against the Strategic Imperatives. The key question should be:

Does this existing project directly support the delivery of our strategic objectives?

If not, kill it and redeploy the assets towards strategic objectives.

Chapter 6:
SILOS ARE GREAT FOR MISSILES, BUT NOT FOR ORGANIZATIONS

*Nothing is more dangerous than an idea
when it is the only one you have.*
~ Emile Charter

A large percentage of strategy execution failures are the result of executives and managers spending more time focusing on their functional objectives than the overall strategic objectives. What is commonly known as *'Silo Focus'*.

It's not that these executives aren't committed to the success of the company, they just aren't aligned on the strategy! By alignment at the top we mean the majority of the time, energy and focus of the senior team, both collectively and as individuals, is on the successful delivery of an enterprise-wide set of strategic objectives. In most organizations, however, strategic alignment at the top is not the case. The *'normal'* in most organizations is that the attention of the leadership team is largely focused on their individual departmental or functional objectives and budgets. Their silos! Their kingdoms! Their empires! Their people! Their projects!

Even when the intent of the meeting is strategic, operational problems quickly hijack the agenda and budget issues because that is what most executives are concerned about, and most comfortable dealing with. Strategy is about the future and the solutions are not always clear. Besides, we've got real problems, right now!

When members of the senior team are more focused on their departmental objectives and budgets, any sort of collaboration quickly deteriorates into a *'win-lose negotiation'* around scarce resources and budgets. With the heavy silo-focus that is common in most organizations it is easy to see why turf battles and inter-departmental squabbles are so common, and why the focus on delivering departmental agendas can easily subvert overall strategy execution. As a result, the CEO often feels like a 'referee', trying to get the senior team to work together.

Breaking the Silos

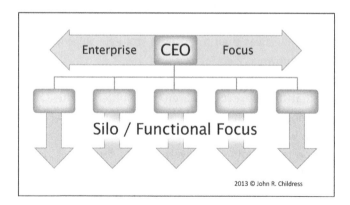

As a result of heavy silo-focus, the CEO is about the only individual who has a horizontal, enterprise-wide perspective (often in tandem with the CFO). Everyone else's attention is focused downward on maximizing their functional operations and meeting functional budgets.

In my experience one of the key requisites for successful strategy execution is to realign the attention and focus of the senior team onto the strategic objectives as opposed to their functional objectives.

In other words, the job of the senior team must be redefined in terms of the delivery of the business strategy.

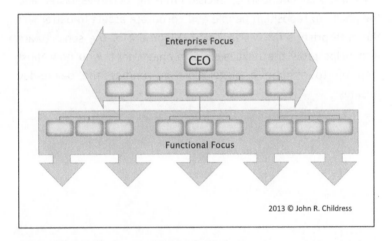

This refocusing of the role of the senior team has two key advantages. First it puts those who have the most authority at the center of the strategy delivery process. So when a problem with a specific strategic initiative is discovered, the focus of the entire senior team is on fixing the problem, rather than the usual approach of endless meetings called by the Program Management Office to coordinate between groups and recommend a solution, which then must go upstairs for approval, to result in another set of meetings. Resulting in the wasting of precious time.

Time is the enemy of a competitive strategy.

The second advantage in making the senior team accountable for the strategy, instead of departmental objectives, is that it naturally leads to a reduction in the size of the senior team, something all CEOs struggle with. In the normal silo-focused organization everyone wants to be on the senior team so their department will be well represented, especially at budget time! Everyone is looking out for their own silo and not the overall enterprise.

By shrinking the senior team to a few key decision makers whose job it is to support the delivery of the strategy across all organizational boundaries, decision-making becomes faster and the ability to reposition people and corporate assets to better suit the enterprise is far easier. This realignment of the senior team also helps grow the next layer of management, who now must step up to assume a bigger role in running the day-to-day business.

SECTION TWO:
WHAT'S THE PLAN, STAN?

Thirty-five years of strategy and organization change consulting experiences, with numerous companies in multiple industries, along with a pragmatic understanding of the principles of lean and six sigma, leadership dynamics and organization change have led us to develop a radically new approach to strategy deployment – which we have come to call *FASTBREAK Strategy Execution.*

In essence, this is a team-driven set of actions, with supporting strategy roadmaps, templates and robust business processes, to align, focus, deploy, govern, communicate and engage the entire organization on delivering strategic outcomes . . . fast!

It was amazing to me when I first got involved in business consulting back in the 1970s how few companies actually had a defined process for strategy execution. And unfortunately, not much has changed. Those few who have either developed or found a useful strategy deployment process stand out not only in how engaged employees are in the business, but also how well they deliver on what they say they are going to do as a business and how they keep ahead of the competition. They aren't any smarter or better funded than their competition. They just deliver.

To put a final punctuation point to this section, in a survey recently conducted by the Balanced Scorecard Collaborative (BSCol), 143 professional performance managers were asked to describe their performance management programs. 70% of those organizations that had a formal strategy execution process in place reported superior performance over other companies in their peer group. Among organizations that had no formal strategy execution process, only 27% reported industry-leading results [19].

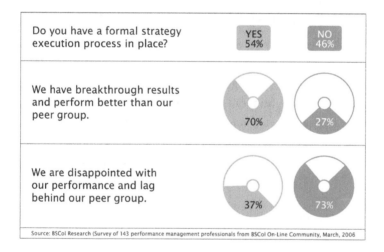

Source: BSCol Research (Survey of 143 performance management professionals from BSCol On-Line Community, March, 2006

Do you have a formal strategy execution process? If you don't, let's explore how to build one. If you already have a formal process in place, then let's work to make it even better!

Chapter 7:
THE NEED FOR SPEED

I feel a need for speed.
~ Tom Cruise as Maverick in Top Gun

Speed has become one of the critical success factors for modern organizations. In the recent past we knew our few competitors and their strengths and weaknesses. Today, globalization and the rapid growth of the developing BRIC (Brazil, Russia, India, China) countries, combined with technology breakthroughs that shatter old business models, keep most CEOs awake at night worrying about the competitors they don't yet know. And there are lots of them. I estimate that in any given industry, you probably have 30-50% more competitors than you know about. And one of them is aiming to be a *'giant killer'*. Speed of delivery is one of the defenses against these unseen and unknown forces. Get to the market first, win market share and then keep innovating, fast. The race is always on!

Money loves speed!
~ Dan Kennedy

The need for speed also forces organizations to think and plan differently. In today's volatile and uncertain global economic marketplace, traditional long term planning (5+ years) must give way to more dynamic and flexible approaches, what I call strategic agility. In this view of strategy an uncertain business environment calls for frequent updates on market conditions, economic assumptions, competitor strengths and weaknesses, and shifts in consumer behavior, which in turn call for adjustments in the business strategy. What is required is not a static strategy execution process, but a dynamic one.

How fast can your organization shift its focus? Where would you start? Would you know where to go to pinpoint the one or two strategic elements of your overall business strategy that must change due to marketplace changes? Most organizations flounder in these situations and as a result, they tend to respond either too late or not boldly enough to capitalize on the situation. The CEO needs a simple way to quickly locate the initiatives that need to change.

Car Wars

Several years ago a major division of a global automobile company found itself at the end of a stretch of 10 CEOs in twelve years, numerous failed strategies, a $1.5 billion loss and declining market share.

When the new CEO arrived he discovered they had the foundation in place for an effective turnaround plan. Since speed was of the essence and he recognized the great amount of talent and experience that existed in the senior team, he decided the most effective approach was getting them to work better together and focus, as a leadership team, on execution. While difficult at first due to suspicion and trust issues, the senior team soon realized each member had significant and different insights into the problems and that they all wanted the same outcome: a healthy company.

Using a visual strategy execution framework, they were able to create a robust *'strategy-on-a-page'* (depicting a house with foundation, pillars and roof) that displayed all the important elements of their turnaround plan and how they fit together. It became a visual representation of the teamwork required to deliver on their business goals. Linked to this visual plan were project statements and milestone plans, metrics, objectives, and KPIs. Plus each member of the team signed up to be accountable for one or more of the strategic initiatives.

During the ensuing year they worked together as an enterprise leadership team; focusing on making effective and quick decisions to build momentum. At the end of the first year they broke even and the second year delivered a $1 billion profit, as well as an increase in market share.

One of the key lessons from this example is the importance of transparency in times where speed is critical to success. To make the best decisions quickly, for the benefit of the enterprise as a whole, everyone needs to know all the information and have a clear line of sight from objectives to plans to metrics to outcomes.

Secondly, by breaking the historical focus on functional objectives and refocusing the senior team on enterprise-wide objectives, information and resources previously held tightly inside functional silos could be quickly moved around the enterprise and used where required. It became commonplace for them to take engineers or manufacturing experts from one location and second them to another location to solve a problem that was slowing down the delivery of a company-wide strategic objective.

And the third big lesson learned was the power of having the entire turnaround strategy on a single page in visual format. This became an important tool in getting the next levels of management engaged in helping deliver on the strategy. Their 'strategy house' became a communication vehicle for all managers and was updated frequently to show the progress against plan.

In this one example we find all the ingredients of the **FASTBREAK Strategy Execution** process: leadership alignment, culture change towards more openness and transparency, and a visual 'plan-on-a-page' roadmap to both communicate and guide the business turnaround.

Chapter 8:

INTRODUCING THE STRATEGY-ON-A-PAGE
EXECUTION ROADMAP

I took the road less traveled by, and that has made all the difference. ~ Robert Frost

The **FASTBREAK Strategy Execution** process is a unique combination of leadership, culture and performance management that seamlessly combines both hard and soft skills (head and heart, process analytics and human psychology) into a robust and effective business process. A significant element of the **FASTBREAK Strategy Execution** process is the Strategy-on-a-Page Execution Roadmap where the entire business strategy is laid out in visual format on a single sheet of paper, or better yet, an interactive computer screen or iPad.

Readers already experienced in strategy execution may note that there are several strategy roadmaps and deployment templates currently on the market from a variety of vendors, some of whom have excellent operation improvement backgrounds and others who are software and technology-based companies.

Most of these products and their consulting processes are based on the same sound business execution principles as you will find in this guidebook.

However, we have built the **FASTBREAK Strategy Execution** process to include several critical elements missing in most other approaches. These important elements are leadership team alignment, culture change and an understanding of human behavior and organization dynamics, without which the mechanics of strategy execution don't function properly.

2013 © John R. Childress

The principles and fundamentals of the **Strategy-on-a-Page Execution Roadmap** are loosely based on the concepts of *hoshin kanri*[20] or Policy Deployment, developed in Japan by Dr. Yoji Akao [21], a co-founder of the Quality Function Deployment Institute and a 1978 recipient of the coveted Deming Prize. Whereas most strategic plans come in thick binders filled with hundreds of charts and graphs and are rarely seen outside the office of the head of strategy, the **Strategy-on-a-Page** makes the execution process easy to visualize and communicate to all levels of the organization, thus enabling better understanding and buy-in among all employees.

The structure and discipline of the Strategy-on-a-Page helps an organization:

- Focus on a few critical breakthrough objectives that define the forward strategy
- Communicate those objectives to all employees
- Involve all leadership in planning to achieve the goal
- Hold participants accountable for achieving their part of the plan

Using insights from behavioral science on how people learn, we have devised this execution process to deliver information on goals, objectives, metrics, strategic initiatives and executive accountability through a variety of information channels (video, customer feedback, spreadsheets, fish-bone diagrams, cause and effect maps, root cause analyses, business stories, charts and graphs). Thus the **Strategy-on-a-Page** is more like a living tapestry of interconnected information than a static strategy binder or a 60-slide PowerPoint presentation. Imagine using your computer mouse to click on any of the areas of the Strategy-on-a-Page to reveal more and more detailed information. This single **Strategy-on-a-Page** and the information connected to it has the capability to align, focus, deploy, govern, communicate and engage the entire organization is delivering strategic outcomes - fast!

The **Strategy-on-a-Page** is built and delivered through senior executive workshops, team meetings, strategic reviews, internal intranet information portals and large-scale engagement events cascading quickly to the entire organization. In this manner the entire organization can be exposed to the key business strategies and how they all fit together to drive the success of the company.

Understanding the Strategy-on-a-Page Format

To fulfill your vision, you must have
hindsight, insight and foresight.

The format is loosely based on the principle of line-of-sight where linking relationships can be easily seen from high-level objectives to lower level goals, showing all the linkages in between.

On a single page the key elements of your company strategy are linked together to allow the entire strategy to be viewed and understood as an overall integrated plan. The elements are arranged as shown below, where the arrows show direct linkages and provide for line-of-sight between all components.

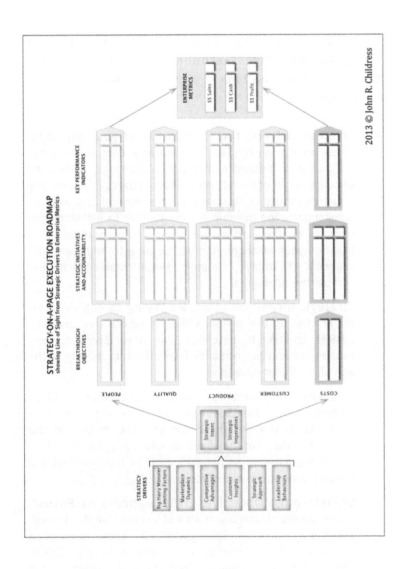

Ingredients in the Strategy-on-a-Page Execution Roadmap

Here is a quick walk through and description of each element in the **Strategy-on-a-Page Execution Roadmap**. We will dive into more detail on how to build your own strategy roadmap in later chapters.

- **Strategy Drivers; the Foundation of your Strategy**: These are the key fundamental analytics, data, information, insights and behaviors that define the logic behind an effective business and competitive strategy. As in any structure (house or skyscraper) if the foundation is weak or substandard, the building will not be able to withstand the rigors of weather and normal usage. The same is definitely true for your strategy. It must be able to withstand the vagaries of today's dynamic global marketplace and competitive pressures.

- **Strategic Intent; What are we Trying to Achieve and Why?**: This is the overall vision of where the company desires to be. It describes the new direction, new capabilities and performance levels desired, usually at the end of a 3-5 year time span.

- **Strategic Imperatives; Define the Key Critical Requirements for Success**: These are the 2 or 3 Big Ticket items that will have the greatest impact on the business if they can get fixed or effectively implemented. Unless these issues get handled, it will be nearly impossible to move further on your strategy.

- **Breakthrough Objectives; Where Should we Focus?**: These are the critical few macro objectives that if achieved, will deliver on the Strategic Intent. These are often segregated into categories. For example: People, Safety, Costs, Customers, Quality, Products and Delivery. Each organization can decide for themselves what their balanced set of Breakthrough Objective categories should be.

- **Strategic Initiatives; How are we going to Deliver the Breakthrough Objectives?**: To deliver Business

Objectives, the company needs to invest in specific projects and strategic initiatives, each supported by full project plans, cost-benefits assessments, root-cause determinations, action steps, accountabilities, end-state metrics and monthly milestones. Only projects that are linked directly to the delivery of a Key Business Objective should be funded.

- **Accountability; Who, exactly, is Responsible for the Success of the Strategic Initiatives?**: Too often, projects and strategic initiatives are passed down several levels to a program manager. While this person may have good program management skills, they usually lack the organizational authority to overcome politics or policy barriers that get in the way, leading to numerous meetings trying to influence senior management to implement changes.

  In the **Strategy-on-a-Page** process each member of the senior team takes direct accountability for one or more of the Strategic Initiatives. In many cases we suggest that individual executives choose one or more projects that are outside their functional area of expertise, thus bringing new, cross-functional ideas and thinking to the various initiatives.

- **Key Performance Indicators; How will we Know if we are on Target?**: To track performance against plan, each Breakthrough Objective has one (or more) corresponding End-State Metrics (a final number or target we are trying to achieve) as well as monthly milestones (again, quantifiable metrics) to track progress against plan each month.

- **Enterprise Metrics; How Well is this Company Performing?**: Most organizations have a small number of overall metrics to determine their performance. These are usually things like actual Revenue/month vs. plan, Profit vs. plan, cash vs. plan, customer satisfaction, etc. Somewhere between 3 and 5 is usually the number that most companies use.

Keeping Score: The Governance of Strategy Execution

If it doesn't matter who wins or loses,
then why do they keep score? ~ Vince Lombardi

When a **Strategy-on-a-Page Execution Roadmap** has been fully developed, it contains all the top-level strategic information necessary to provide managers and employees with an integrated view of the business strategy and an understanding of how all the elements are linked. An important element of the **Strategy-on-a-Page** format is the use of a *'traffic light'* system for focused governance of the overall Enterprise Metrics, Key Performance Indicators and the Strategic Initiatives.

What makes the **Strategy-on-a-Page Execution Roadmap** unique is the fact that each cell can be connected to a database of the appropriate information necessary for understanding the situation in more detail, to help with employee communication, team problem solving, innovation discussions, and regular governance.

Behind the **Strategy-on-a-Page** lies a wealth of information hyperlinked to spreadsheets, PowerPoint templates, business plans, customer intelligence, data on marketplace trends, etc. which all link together, turning the **Strategy-on-a-Page** into a living tapestry of management information and an important performance management process. Clicking on any of the areas reveals the appropriate information about those elements of the strategy. Additionally, as the weeks and months progress, information is updated on a regular basis to track progress and to develop a forward look at upcoming issues or concerns in execution.

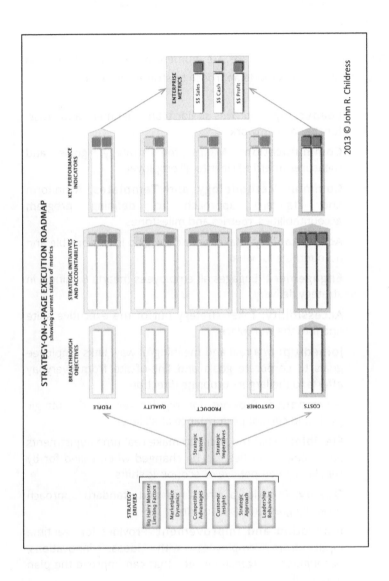

Key Benefits of the Strategy-on-a-Page Execution Roadmap

From our experience there are numerous benefits of such in integrated enterprise-wide approach to strategy execution:

- **Leadership**: Improves senior team alignment and cross-functional teamwork
- **Communication**: Makes the strategy, goals and measures (metrics) clear to all employees
- **Common Methodology and Templates**: A uniform and standard approach to defining program accountabilities, metrics and milestones
- **Accountability**: Makes very clear who is responsible and accountable for what
- **Engagement**: Engages all employees (hearts & minds) in strategy delivery
- **Accessibility**: Takes strategy out of the executive suite and into the workplace
- **Joined-up:** In a real and meaningful way, links employee goals to corporate goals and line-of-site from everyday efforts to the larger corporate direction
- **Governance**: Provides for regular review of strategic goals and current performance at all levels
- **Flexible:** Instills the ability to make real-time adjustments so strategic activities can be changed when called for by regulatory, competitive or economic shifts
- **Quality**: Provides a structured and standard approach ensuring greater quality control
- **Innovation and Improvement**: Provides for real-time input from employees with ideas, innovations, observations, suggestions, etc. that can improve the plan and results.

Chapter 9:
A REAL 'ROADMAP'

If you take the meat ax to the problem, you destroy
relationships. And who loses? The employees.
The customers. And the shareholders.
~ Gordon Bethune, CEO Continental Airlines

In 1994 Continental Airlines was on the brink of its third bankruptcy in less than a decade, was dead last in every airline performance statistic (and had been for the past 10 years), had a track record of 10 straight years of losing money, endured repeated union strikes and slow-downs, and at one point only had 60 days of cash left. Yet they successfully turned around an obviously broken company by focusing everyone on a set of joined up initiatives and objectives.

I have taken the liberty of putting the Continental plan as it existed in 1994 into the **Strategy-on-a-Page Execution Roadmap** template as an example. (There are many other more current examples, but needless to say, most of them are company confidential, so we will use this one now that Continental and United have merged and have a new strategy).

The roadmap reads from far left, the Strategy Drivers, into the main focus (Strategic Intent and Strategic Imperatives), which determine the Breakthrough Objectives in four categories (People, Product, Marketplace, Financial), which link to Strategic Initiatives and Key Performance Indicators, which then deliver the Enterprise Metrics.

As you can see, a simple, easy to follow, easy to communicate, and easy to manage line-of-sight strategy map.

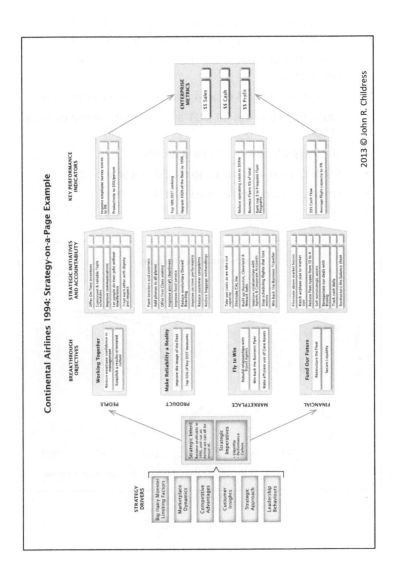

Continental Airlines 1994: **Strategy-on-a-Page Example**

2013 © John R. Childress

And the results?

- Continental Airlines returned to profitability in 1995, the first year after the new strategy was implemented
- 1996: Voted airline of the year, against 300 global competitors
- Ranked in the top 5 of all global airlines ever since 1996
- Among the top 4 in all DOT airline service statistics since 1996
- 16 straight quarters of record profits
- Share price rose from $3.30 to $50 in 4 years
- Employee turnover reduced by 45%

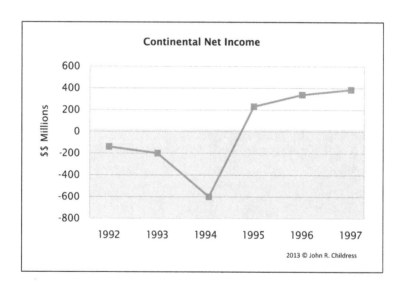

SECTION THREE:
BUILDING YOUR STRATEGY-ON-
A-PAGE EXECUTION ROADMAP

What's the use of running if you're not on the right road?
~ Old German Proverb

Why Are We Here?

Over time businesses tend to lose the ability to articulate who they really are and what they stand for, mostly because the early excitement and newness of the challenge of startup and survival give way to a focus on spreadsheets, ratios, sales quotas and EBITDA. In addition, successive changes in leadership tend to dull the clarity of purpose held by the founders.

A very real example is Goldman Sachs, the full-service global investment banking and securities firm which provides mergers and acquisitions advice, underwriting services, asset management, and prime brokerage to its clients, which include corporations, governments and individuals. The firm also engages in proprietary trading and private equity deals, and is a primary dealer in the United States Treasury security market.

Goldman Sachs is huge: 33,000 employees and revenues in excess of $29 billion. Its name is recognized globally for its financial expertise. At one point Goldman Sachs was the elite financial services firm and regularly recruited the best and brightest from the top MBA schools.

But the elite reputation of the firm is now very much in question. The original corporate culture, based on its famous 14 Business Principles, with 'our client's interests always come first' as the number one principle, has been transformed into that of a *'corporate pirate'* where greed and self-interest have replaced both personal and professional ethics. In fact, the common name for Goldman Sachs nowadays is the *'Vampire Squid'*, a nod to its blood-sucking greed and global reach.

Recently, a resignation letter by Greg Smith [22], former head of Goldman Sachs US equity derivatives business, which was published in the New York Times, brought to light the changes in ethics and corporate culture that have taken place over the past 20 years. The day after the publication, $2.5 billion was erased from the firm's balance sheet.

> *To build and execute on a competitive strategy, it is critical to lay a solid foundation based on clarity of purpose and a clear strategic intent.*

Tesco: 12 years of Value Creation and Growth

A good example of clarity of purpose and clear strategic intent can be seen in the competitive world of UK supermarkets between 1995 and 2007, when Tesco consistently outgrew and outperformed its two peers, Sainsbury and Marks & Spencer [23].

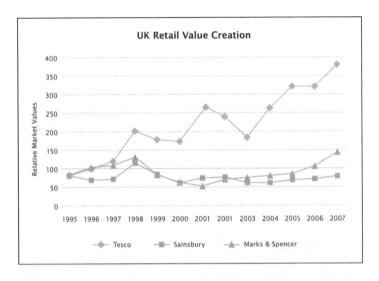

As of 2011 Tesco is the 3rd largest global retailer with 440,000+ people worldwide, £51.8 billion in revenue, and 3,728 stores worldwide. As the following graph shows, in 1995 Tesco, along with Marks & Spencer and Sainsbury were all about the same size. Yet Tesco clearly outdistanced both its UK competitors and has become one of the top global retailers.

How did this come about? The executives at Tesco are convinced that having a clear purpose, vision and strategy, along with aligned objectives, metrics, initiatives and senior team alignment and accountabilities all worked together to create the focus, alignment and discipline required to achieve these outstanding results. And importantly, they stressed a balanced approach, seeking excellence in all areas, but especially for their own staff and for customer service.

They also developed their own version of a *strategy execution wheel*, which became the major tool they used to manage and run the Tesco business for years. Each segment of their strategy wheel, customer, community, operations, people, finance, had clear statements of purpose and cascading metrics that all employees could understand.

Today, however, Tesco is struggling to maintain its dominant market position as well as its once loyal customers. Have they forgotten their core purpose? Are they concentrating too much on price and costs and not enough on people and customer? Seems like their 'strategy execution wheel' is definitely out of balance.

> *Where your talent and the needs of the world cross,*
> *therein lies your purpose.*
> *~ Roy Spence, co-founder, IdeaCity*

Enduring Purpose

In 1961 US President John F. Kennedy called for hundreds of millions of dollars to fund a space program to get the first man on the Moon by 1970. *"I believe that this nation should commit itself to achieving the goal, before this decade is out, of landing a man on the Moon and returning him safely to Earth."* [24]

On 21 July 1969, right on schedule, Neil Armstrong became the first man to set foot on the Moon. The clear purpose contained in this speech, and the national fervor it created (with a little help from the Russian launch of Sputnik and Uri Gagarin) galvanized the focus of the scientific community and significantly expanded the scope and funding of the National Aeronautics and Space Administration (NASA). But rather than just a one mission endeavor, the leading scientists of the day had a much bigger view and established for NASA an *'Enduring Purpose'* that would guide it well into the 21st Century.

NASA's Enduring Purpose describes its reason for being as follows:

> *"To pioneer the future in space exploration,*
> *scientific discovery and aeronautics research."*

Whether it is the Mars space probe, Pioneer 10, the Space Shuttle, the Manned Space Station, the Apollo Moon program or the Mars Curiosity Rover, each of these missions had a defined strategy, but all fulfilled the enduring purpose of NASA.

Ask most people on the street the purpose of business and they will likely answer: *"To make money, of course."* But with a deeper understanding of commerce and enterprise, it quickly becomes clear that making money is a by-product of providing goods and services that people want and will pay for.

Every business begins with a purpose, a reason for being, and before you can build and effectively execute a strategy you must get in touch again with your organization's Enduring Purpose. Chances are good that it has been lost over time and even if it is still remembered, it rarely remains as the driving force of the business.

Here are some questions that you and the senior team can work on to help clarify Enduring Purpose (word-smiting and catchy phrases are not the goal here, just a shared understanding of who we are and why we exist as an organization). This is the first set of discussions we engage the senior executive team in when starting the **FASTBREAK Strategy Execution** process, long before they begin to talk about goals, objectives, or strategic initiatives.

How well can your leadership team answer these questions? What about your employees?

- Why was the business started in the first place?
- What were the original values and business proposition?
- What empty niche did the business aim to fill when it was founded?
- What customer need(s) did we start out to satisfy?

- What did we offer the market that was unique?

- How would you define the Enduring Purpose of your organization today?

- As a leadership team, what do we (deeply) believe, hold sacred and share in common about this business and its purpose?

Strategies change to match the changing marketplace threats, but understanding your organization's enduring purpose is critical to engaging both minds and hearts.

> We tend to think we can separate strategy from culture, but we fail to notice that in most organizations strategic thinking is deeply colored by tacit assumptions about who they are and what their mission is.
> ~ Edgar Schein, professor MIT Sloan School of Management

Chapter 10:
I WANT . . .

I want to put a ding in the universe.
~ Steve Jobs

We are often asked by a CEO client:

> *Where do I start with all this strategy and execution*
> *stuff? There are so many critically important*
> *factors. Do I gather customer data, marketplace*
> *data and trends, competitor assessments, culture*
> *surveys? Do I start with assessing the skills of the*
> *senior team?*

The answer is that all these are critical and important, but they are secondary. From our experience, strategy and strategy execution begins inside the heart, ambitions and desires of the CEO, the one person who has the broadest view of the organization and the market. While most executives in the organization are focused on functional issues and goals, the CEO has the job of seeing and understanding the big picture; how the organization as a whole fits into the marketplace, the competitive landscape, customer segments, and the community.

Rather than develop a lofty *'vision'* statement, usually crafted by the PR department and hung up on walls, it is more effective, and more believable for the CEO to develop a series of *'I want . . .'* statements. And the CEO must be passionate about them.

My father used to have a saying in our family: *"If Momma ain't happy, nobody's happy!"* This little phrase helped me avoid getting deeper into trouble as a kid, and also sheds some light on strategy execution as well. I've seen what were supposedly excellent strategies fail miserably and result in the firing of the CEO. And I've also seen extremely risky strategies succeed and transform a mediocre company into a world-class quality leader.

So, I have developed a rule of thumb about CEOs and strategy execution. It goes like this:

> *The greater the pain and discomfort of the CEO, the higher the probability of successful execution!*

After all these years I can pretty much tell, 15 minutes into a conversation with a CEO, the likely success of his/her strategic agenda. Some give eloquent presentations, others even rant, but unless there is a seriously high level of discomfort inside the CEO, not much will change. But when the inner pain and discomfort of the CEO gets high enough, then I tend to wager on a successful outcome.

What's your level of resolve concerning strategy and strategy execution? What's your personal and professional level of resolve? What triggers your *'burning platform'* or *'special opportunity'* moments?

I have a feeling that discomfort, resolve and commitment are linked together. My advice to most CEOs is: *"Get committed and get your courage up, or stop talking about change!"*

We often use this chart in our early conversation with a client:

It is up to the CEO to translate their commitment and resolve into a clear picture of the future, with specific stretch goals and targets. Rather than develop a lofty 'vision' statement, it is more effective, and more believable, to describe the way forward in a series of *'I want . . .'* statements. The trick in developing a useful set of *'I want'* statements is to make certain they are both challenging and achievable.

The *'I want . . .'* statements should be both simple and at the same time compelling. It should be clear to everyone exactly what the CEO is demanding from the organization. And they should encompass issues such as financial, costs, people, culture, customers, etc. (This initial *'I want . . .'* thinking is critical as the foundation for developing Breakthrough Objectives – see Chapter 16).

Here is an example:

The head of a large pharmaceutical division came up with just four '*I want*' statements, but they were bold enough to help propel his organization to new heights.

- I want us to keep score and post it for our associates to see
- I want everyone to be given the opportunity to provide input that is listened to and acted upon.
- I want manufacturing costs to decrease by 5% or more each year for the next four years.
- I want us to keep asking why.

To assist you in developing your '*I want . . .*' statements, use the following to organize your thinking.

- I want (financial)
- I want (quality)
- I want (customers or customer experience)
- I want (culture)
- I want (costs)
- I want (products)
- I want (leadership team)

You can easily come up with your own key categories, but remember, without your commitment and passion, they will just be sound bites and carry little emotional power or positive energy.

Once you have thought about it and set down a few drafts, it is important to include you direct reports in your thinking. Allow them to question and challenge your '*I want . . .*' statements. This process will not only engage them, but also elevate your thinking to an even higher level. But don't allow this process to fall into the spiral of unending debates and word-smithing. After all, these are things you about which you are passionate and committed, so make a stand.

Get up, stand up, Stand up for your rights.
Get up, stand up, Don't give up the fight.
~ Bob Marley

Chapter 11:
How Do We Make Money? -
Understanding The Current Business Model

Rule No.1: Never lose money.
Rule No.2: Never forget rule No.1.
~ Warren Buffett

This may be a bold statement, but I am willing to bet that very few on your senior team can fully articulate your current business model. In other words, the map that describes the major interactions and factors affecting how your organization delivers value to customers and turns effort and costs into profit. Throughout my 35 years of working with senior executive teams I have been appalled at how few fully understand the business model. They readily understand how their individual function works, but few understand the full business model.

And why is this important? Because, one of the first places to look for insights into effective strategy development and execution is the existing business model. By mapping out the process of the current business model, then stepping back and looking at it critically (seeing the forest instead of the trees) it often happens that insights pop out.

For example, with one supplier of heavy truck components, after reviewing their current business model it became obvious to everyone that the organization was not spending enough time with its customers, treating them more like a transaction than an on-going business partner. The model also pointed out that plans for expanding into developing markets was hampered by lack of market intelligence.

Often we find that current business models have not kept up with either the changing global economy, shifts in technology, or customer evolution. This insight is critical for the senior team to understand and debate. I am not suggesting that mapping out the current business model will lead to a radical change in how a company goes to market, but will certainly point out areas of weakness in the current operations that an improved strategy and more effective strategy execution can overcome.

You don't have a real strategy if it doesn't pass these two tests: that what you're planning to do really matters to your existing and potential customers; and second, it differentiates you from your competition. ~ Gary Hamel

Chapter 12:
THE BIG HAIRY MONSTER AND LIMITING FACTORS

Strategy coordinates action to address a specific challenge.
~ Richard Rumelt

Before the analytics, research, market studies, customer feedback, and strategic choices, it is critical to be clear on the problem. What we call the **Big Hairy Monster** that is causing your company grief, or is about to have you for lunch.

One of the biggest mistakes in strategy execution is to try to improve everything! The reality is, we all have limited budgets, limited time and never enough talent. And to be honest, there are and will always be inefficiencies and business problems, no matter how great our market share or how high the profit margin.

While a good CEO does not shy away from continuous improvement, a competitive strategy is not continuous improvement. It's a step change. A strategy is a coordinated set of actions to overcome a specific (imminent or impending) challenge.

There will always be room for continuous improvement and at times, continuous improvement projects can help deliver parts of a competitive advantage, such as cost reduction or speed to market. But if the Big Hairy Monster has you for lunch, continuous improvement is immaterial.

The key question for determining your Big Hairy Monster and the most critical threat to the success of your business is:

What is the one thing that could put us out of business in the next 3-5 years?

Believe it or not, most organizations forget to ask this simple, yet profound question. Instead they focus on goals, mission statements, visions, aspirations and the like. All these are important, as you will see in the next few chapters on Strategic Choices. But unless you can clearly identify the one real threat to your organization in the next 3-5 years, you will have a lofty vision and a dead business.

The Big Hairy Monster facing Alan Mulally, new CEO of Ford, in 2006 was subtle. Nearly every automotive manufacturing leader believed the threat to their business was low cost, high quality foreign cars entering the US market. And with an economic slowdown, consumers were wary of spending too much on a new car. Thus this interpretation of the Big Hairy Monster drove most automakers to implement a strategy of excessive harmonization, common platforms for multiple brands, and reduced styling differentiation. Actions designed to reduce cost and improve quality. While this was a critical ingredient to fend off the invasion of foreign automakers, it was also costly, especially for those with global operations and multiple brands.

It took Alan Mulally and a few others to determine that while vehicle cost and quality were very important, Ford's Big Hairy

Monster was *"lack of focus"*. In other words, they had some good plans for recovery, but were spread too thin, with a costly mix of luxury and performance brands as well as the traditional Ford offerings. Several years before, Ford had acquired Jaguar, Land Rover, Volvo and Aston Martin (forming the Ford Performance Automotive Group), hoping to capitalize on a growing global economy combined with Ford's automotive expertise and marketing power.

However, in a severe global economic downturn, when cash is at a premium, fighting battles on too many fronts, even with the right strategy, can be a fast road to bankruptcy. Mulally could see clearly that Ford was trying to do too much on too many fronts and didn't have adequate management talent or capital to effectively look after both the traditional Ford product range and the Performance Automotive Group brands. Lewis Booth, Ford CFO, even went on record saying that it would have been a tragedy to starve the PAG brands of resources and let them fade away; far better to find them a new owner who could look after them while the senior team focused on saving the traditional Ford business.

Based on the realization that the Big Hairy Monster for Ford was lack of focus, Mulally and the Ford team sold off Volvo, Jaguar, Land Rover and Aston Martin and concentrated on producing distinctive and stylish Fords, while at the same time lowering costs, refinancing the business, harmonizing where appropriate, and improving quality and fuel efficiency. Had Ford tried to apply its turnaround strategy over all its extended family of product lines, PAG plus Ford-badged vehicles, they quickly would have run out of money and available talent. As a result, Ford was the only one of the Big US automakers to deliver on its turnaround strategy without seeking bankruptcy protection or bailout money.

The point? Identifying your organization's Big Hairy Monster is not easy, but it is critical.

One practical approach to ferreting out your Big Hairy Monster is to get your management teams to come up with what they believe are the Big Hairy Monster *'candidates'*, then have a group meeting to display all the assembled monsters at once. It should quickly become apparent which one rises above all the others. This is also an excellent meeting for surfacing ideas and creating management alignment.

There is another place to look for an answer to the question: *"What is the one thing that could put us out of business in the next 3-5 years?"* Inside your company. Since all organizations are essentially a Value-Chain, with materials coming in one side and products exiting the other, there is always one weak point in the chain. You must find this weak point and address it as a cross-functional team.

The Limiting Factor(s)

Consider the example of a heavy duty off-road axle manufacturer that relies on various suppliers for forgings, castings and engineered products which are shipped into an assembly plant, put together, then finished axles are shipped out to customers around the world. Somewhere along this chain there are one or more limiting factors.

When sales fall off, the answer may not be adding more sales staff if the limiting factor is actually a long lead-time for one of the key components. When the competition is quoting 90-day delivery and you can only deliver in 180 days due to a constraint in the supply of steel housings, even if you add twice as many salesmen and have the best quality, customers who are time constrained will go elsewhere. The only real action is to reduce lead-time to be competitive. Lead-time is the limiting factor in this situation. Then if you want to gain market share, improve the sales process.

With the Big Hairy Monster clearly identified and an understanding of limiting factors, it's now time to build the foundation for competitive advantage, which will then drive your strategy and execution actions.

Chapter 13:
THE NECESSARY FOUNDATION FOR COMPETITIVE COMBAT

In God we trust; all others must bring data. ~ W. Edwards Deming

An effective strategy, and an effective strategy roadmap, must rest on a solid foundation of insight, information, wants, needs, and real data. Whether you do a formal SWOT analysis (Strengths-Weaknesses-Opportunities-Threats), or any of the other competitive strategy assessments, it is critical to understand the fundamentals of where the market is currently, and even more importantly, where it is headed. It is also important to take an honest look at your own organizational capabilities, as they will influence the pace at which a competitive strategy can be implemented.

The building of a **Strategy-on-a-Page Execution Roadmap** begins with an assessment of the external and internal environment, what we call the Strategic Drivers. While you can choose to use different names for these various cells of information, it is critical that this information be gathered and discussed prior to formulating your forward strategy.

> *All men can see these tactics whereby I conquer, but what none can see is the strategy out of which victory is evolved.* ~ Sun Tzu

Marketplace Dynamics

> *It ain't what you don't know that gets you into trouble. It's what you know for sure that just ain't so.* ~ Mark Twain

What is happening in your marketplace? What might be just over the horizon that could significantly impact your company's competitive position? Do you know? Or do you just think you know? Where's the data to back up your hunches?

What happens outside the walls of your organization is far more important than what happens internally. Unless you are constantly scanning the marketplace for shifts and changes, it is easy to lose ground by being occupied on internal issues. And the further you slip behind in this fast changing global business environment, the more difficult it is to catch up

In what direction is regulation moving? Is your marketplace reaching a growth plateau? How could current world events impact your marketplace? In what ways can technology or innovation disrupt your plans?

Many retail and service organizations missed one of the fundamental marketplace shifts in the past several decades. The 'graying of the consumer population' and the growing market for older generation goods and services. The over-50 market has grown into a major economic and consumer force [25], currently estimated at $3 trillion (yes, trillion) in annual consumer spending (by only 30% of the population) and over 50% of consumer spending in every vertical – especially health care.

We strongly urge you and your senior team to spend time, regularly, talking about and researching the marketplace dynamics in your industry, because that's where the money is going.

Competitive Analysis

If you don't have a competitive advantage, don't compete.
~ Jack Welch

As a business grows, so does its competition. Your success invites hungry competitors to enter your market. Competitors want a chunk of successful businesses and they are driven to figure out how to make their products better and cheaper, and how to win over your customers.

Out of the assessment of your current and potential competition should come the ability to determine your current competitive advantages and weaknesses.

Once you have a fairly complete understanding of who your current and potential competitors are and how they stack up against your organization, this information should be summarized and discussed among the management team to draw any and all insights and information that can be used to guide the development of your strategy.

Customer Insight

There is nothing so terrible as activity without insight.
~Johan Wolfgang von Goethe

In working with senior teams and assisting in strategy execution and turnarounds, I have found a single surprising fact. Most companies who struggle with growth have very little real understanding of their customer wants and needs. They have lots of *'tribal knowledge'* and *'beliefs'* about what the customer wants, but very little actual data. And in my experience, those who make customer decisions on past history (old information) and tribal knowledge (Bill has sold to that client for years, he knows what they want) are ripe for a competitor who truly understands the customer.

The opposite is also the case; those with real time data and information on customers (buying habits, preferences, etc.) tend to deliver consistent growth. Walmart grew at a phenomenal rate for three decades on the back of a technology infrastructure that delivered daily sales and customer buying information gathered from all stores and all regions, allowing the buyers to adjust their buying mix based on real-time data and sales trends. Knowing the customer allows you to deliver products and services that fit customer wants and needs faster than the competition.

Strategic Approach

Lead, follow, or get the hell out of the way.
~ Gen. George Patton

There is not enough cash, resources, capabilities, skills or time to compete on all fronts and be good at them all. To be successful in building and delivering on a competitive strategy, choices need to be made as to where to expend capital and energy.

Fred Crawford, currently CEO of Alix Partners, and Ryan Matthews wrote a ground breaking book on the subject of strategic approach: *The Myth of Excellence: Why Great Companies Never Try to be Best at Everything (Crawford et al, 2003)*.

Based on exhaustive research, *The Myth of Excellence* proves the futility of trying to be excellent in all aspects of a commercial transaction:

- Price
- Product
- Access
- Experience
- Service

Instead, they wisely suggest the best strategic approach is to dominate on one element, differentiate on a second, and be at industry par (or better) on the rest.

Walmart, the largest retailer in the world, is a great example of an organization with a clearly defined strategic approach. Of the five commercial elements above, Walmart has clearly chosen to dominate on Price and be the low-cost price leader. Even their advertising reflects this focus. They have chosen to differentiate, but not dominate, on Access. Their stores carry just about everything a consumer would want all in one place. No driving all over town to do your shopping.

At Walmart you can get clothes, fishing tackle, washing machines, peanut butter, milk, beer and wine, drugs, groceries, gardening essentials, just about everything. They also differentiate themselves from the competition by using technology to gain easy access to up-to-date information on sales, customer trends, fast moving items, etc. in order to keep the right products in front of their customers. And Walmart stays pretty much at industry par on the other three: Product, Experience and Service.

Apple, the most valuable company on the planet, has chosen to dominate on Product. They focus a massive amount of effort, time and money on their products, making them easy to use, esthetically pleasing and *"cool"*, with superior technology, and user-friendly functionality. You can tell an apple product in one glance. Apple then chooses to differentiate on Service. The Mac stores are always packed as people know that the staff are well trained, can answer (and will answer) any and all questions and are eager to be helpful. Contrast this to the Dell or HP hotline for customer service. And concerning the other three elements; Access, Experience and Price, Apple is at or above industry par.

Just think of how much time, effort and money it would take Walmart or Apple to become world-class in all five elements: Price, Product, Access, Experience and Service? Not a winning strategy.

Think hard about your strategic approach and don't fall for the myth of excellence in all things. Choose where and how you can dominate and then make certain you Execute, Execute, Execute.

Chapter 14:
TALK IS CHEAP, SO ARE VALUE STATEMENTS - FOCUS ON BEHAVIORS AND GROUND RULES INSTEAD

Talk is cheap, except when Congress does it. ~ Cullen Hightower

In the mid-1980s after the publication of *In Search of Excellence*, an army of consultants burst on the scene to help *'rudderless'* organizations build mission and vision statements, which seemed to then require the need for values and value statements to guide the culture into alignment with the new vision. (Whew! Even I get tired of management speak).

Even Enron had printed values and lofty statements [26], which of course no one paid any attention to, as is the case in most organizations.

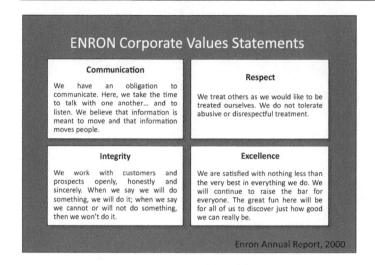

ENRON Corporate Values Statements

Communication

We have an obligation to communicate. Here, we take the time to talk with one another... and to listen. We believe that information is meant to move and that information moves people.

Respect

We treat others as we would like to be treated ourselves. We do not tolerate abusive or disrespectful treatment.

Integrity

We work with customers and prospects openly, honestly and sincerely. When we say we will do something, we will do it; when we say we cannot or will not do something, then we won't do it.

Excellence

We are satisfied with nothing less than the very best in everything we do. We will continue to raise the bar for everyone. The great fun here will be for all of us to discover just how good we can really be.

Enron Annual Report, 2000

The Test

Life is a cruel teacher. She gives the test first and the lesson afterwards!

When I give speeches to senior teams or audiences of senior executives, I almost always do this simple test with the group. I first ask: *"How many of you believe that values and value statements are important in running an effective organization?"* All the hands shoot up. I then ask them: *"How many of you work for an organization that has published their values or value statements?"* 90+% of the hands again go up.

Then I ask them all to pull out a piece of blank paper, grab a pen or pencil, and write down the exact values or value statements of their company. As you can imagine, there is a gasp and then a very awkward silence with much fumbling around and shifting in the chairs.

The results? Over the past 30 years the average has been that less than 50% of the audience can actually recall and accurately write down their company values or value statements. And these are the senior executives! I did this recently with a financial services organization in London, which had just 4 simple values. Only one of the 8 senior executives in the room got them all correct!

Why, if values are so important to running effective enterprises, are so few senior executives able to write them down, much less live them day-to-day? My friend Carolyn Taylor describes this difference between words and deeds in her book *Walking the Talk*.

For many companies, value statements are seen as a tick-the-box requirement. *"We should have a set of printed values; they look good on the wall and in the Annual Report."* But if you can't even remember your lofty value statements, how can you really execute on the people and culture dimension of your strategy?

Understanding the Behaviors Required – Ground Rules

Action determines results, but it is behavior that drives action.

While it may seem odd to find behaviors in a section on strategy drivers, the behavior of the leadership team (how they behave and work together, and how they deal with employees, customers, suppliers, partners, etc.) is one of the key ingredients to building and successfully executing a business strategy. While change is easy on paper, it is difficult in practice. And the behavior of the senior team can either add to that difficulty, or help to foster trust, hope, motivation and courage in the workforce.

The simple fact is, employees, all the way up from the shop floor, watch the behavior of the senior team, collectively and as individuals. But they don't just notice the leadership behavior (and it is a big part of every after work conversation and even during working hours), they actually take their clues as to what is important and how to get ahead from watching the behavior of the leadership team.

Organizations are shadows of their leadership . . .
that's the good news and the bad news!

Do members of the senior team fight each other and bad mouth each other, or do they openly support and appreciate their peers? Does the senior team say one thing in speeches and yet behave the opposite? Is cross-functional teamwork really practiced or just talked about?

The successful delivery of any strategic plan is dependent upon the actions and behavior of those tasked with the delivery, which means a lot of employees. It is important for the senior leadership team to understand that the actual delivery of the strategy may require a new set of behaviors to be exhibited within the company. By its very nature a strategic plan is different from business-as-usual objectives and will require both new skills and new behaviors.

And if the senior team doesn't adopt these new
behaviors, employees won't either.

In order to better understand the behaviors that will be required to effectively deliver your strategy, you should look at each of your Breakthrough Objectives (see Chapters 15 & 16 for more on Breakthrough Objectives) and ask your team the following questions:

- If this particular breakthrough objective were successfully delivered, what behaviors would we observe in the company that perhaps didn't exist before?
- What should we do along the journey when we see this type of behavior?
- How should we introduce the fact that these new behaviors will be required from everyone in order to deliver our breakthrough objectives?

- What new behaviors will the senior team have to adopt to support the successful delivery of our strategy?

- What current behavior must we, the senior team, stop doing?

This should touch off a very rich discussion about the leadership behaviors required from the senior team to help support and facilitate the successful delivery of the strategy.

Team Ground Rules

Rather than lofty values statements or flowery descriptions of desired behaviors, we prefer the senior team to come up with their own set of ground rules, using everyday language that everyone can easily understand.

Here is an example of a simple set of Team Ground Rules a senior leadership team in the defense sector uses as guidelines for how they must behave in order to effectively execute their competitive strategy. During every meeting held inside the company, the first item on the agenda is to go through the Team Behaviors and remind everyone in the meeting that these are the 'rules of engagement' for this and every meeting.

- Be Open . . . Use Possibility Thinking
- Be Decisive . . . Do It, Try It, Improve It
- Be Trusting . . . Assume Best Intentions
- No Hidden Agenda . . . Let's Get It All On the Table, Now
- Challenge the Status Quo . . . Ask the 5 Whys
- Be Accountable . . . Take Full Ownership
- Apply the Golden Rule . . . Lead as you would like to be led
- Look Beyond the Horizon . . . Push Our Business into the Future
- Use the Expertise of the Team . . .Solve Problems Together

- No Triangles. Talk Directly To the Person, Not About Them
- Have Fun . . . Enjoy Each Other

We suggest you develop your own set of leadership behaviors, using simple language that everyone can understand, and hold each other accountable.

I meant what I said and I said what I meant. ~ *Dr Seuss*

Chapter 15:
THE TARGET – CLEAR AND SIMPLE

Results are obtained by exploiting opportunities,
not by solving problems. ~ Peter Drucker

Strategic Intent

In working with numerous clients on aligning their current strategic plan so that it could be effectively delivered (as you know most strategies fail due to poor execution), I discovered a considerable amount of confusion and lack of clarity around the terms, *'vision'* and *'mission'* statements. One of the reasons that companies struggle with vision and mission is that these two words tend to be poorly defined and more often than not filled with consultant speak.

What is needed is a more practical and useful definition of just what a vision and mission entails. So in working with the senior executive team at one client we decided to get specific and focus on some simple definitions.

Instead of vision and mission, we decided to use **Strategic Intent** and **Strategic Imperatives** as a way to communicate where the company was headed and what was important.

Strategic Intent refers simply to *'what we want for this company'* and usually has a limited time frame, say 3 years.

For example, during the turnaround at Continental Airlines, the strategic intent was to *"Run a profitable airline we can all be proud of"*. Pretty simple and straightforward, yet powerful when understood and internalized by all employees.

The Ford turnaround engineered and led by Alan Mulally laid out a clear and simple statement of strategic intent: *"One Ford: One Team – One Plan – One Goal."*

Watch any interview in the press or on YouTube with Mulally or any member of the Ford senior team and you will hear their strategic intent repeated over and over. It drives their performance.

Strategic Imperatives

The first and most imperative necessity in war is money, for
money means everything else - men, guns, ammunition.
~ Ida Tarbell

Strategic Imperatives are the 2-3 *'Big Ticket'* items that will
have the greatest impact on the business if they can get fixed or
effectively implemented. Unless these issues get handled, it will be
nearly impossible to move further on your strategy.

Coming back to our example of the Continental Airlines
turnaround, what were those few critical ingredients, the Strategic
Imperatives, which would ensure the delivery of the strategic
intent? Most people think it was access to money since after all this
was a turnaround situation where the company was at that time
$2.5B in default.

But in 1994 Continental was approaching its third bankruptcy in
ten years. Which means they had raised money twice before to get
them out of the hole, only to wind up back there again. So why
should raising more money this time be any different?

Gordon Bethune and Greg Brenneman, the architects and leaders
of the successful turnaround at Continental, realized that their two
strategic imperatives were liquidity and a performance culture.
Liquidity is obvious; keep the doors open. But the surprising
imperative was building a performance culture through
recognition and employee engagement.

After years of successive cost cutting, and command and control
management styles, the employees had become increasingly
negative about the company they worked for. And their negative
attitudes about the company and management led to poor and
often caustic interactions with customers. This downward spiral of
negative behavior got so bad that many employees ripped the

Continental badges off their uniforms so as not to be identified by angry customers.

Continental's biggest strategic imperative was to rebuild employee trust in management and create a performance culture. Without this element in place, none of the other business and financial restructuring would last.

Another example is Apple, whose strategic imperatives are *'cool'* and *'user-friendly'*! Yes they are a consumer technology company and have sophisticated software and chips in their products, as do many other consumer technology companies. But if Apple ever abandoned designing products that were Cool and if their products ever became too technical and unfriendly to use, their massive brand equity would quickly erode.

Apple is the largest sales-per-square-foot retailer in the US [27]. Its sales-per-square-foot are nearly twice that of the organization in second place, Tiffany & Co, the upscale jewelry chain. And demand for Apple's cool, user-friendly apple products is so great that many of its stores are open 24/7. I know lots of retailers who would kill for this type of customer demand.

Figure out what your few key strategic imperatives are, focus on them with a maniacal intent, and they will propel you towards the successful delivery of your strategic intent.

Chapter 16:
SINGLE MALT SCOTCH AND BREAKTHROUGH
THINKING

*Most leaders have no idea of the giant capacity for
performance they can immediately command when they
focus all their organization's resources and attention on a
few key breakthrough objectives.*

When Gordon Bethune first took over at Continental there were so many things broken about the organization it was difficult to decide where to start. After a few weeks of getting around and listening to the issues, he invited Greg Brenneman, his Chief Operating Officer, over to his house one evening. Bethune pulled out a bottle of Scotch and a handful of blank paper.

"What should we go for? What would be truly breakthrough for this company? Let's not spend our energy on incremental fixes, let's think big." At the end of the evening, the bottle was empty and the pages were full of notes, out of which evolved a few critical

'Breakthrough Objectives' that would not only secure a turnaround, but put Continental at the top of the airline league tables and number one in the hearts of customers and employees.

The difference between a business plan and a strategic plan is not just the scope and time scale. Business plans are usually incremental and short term. Strategies are intended to bring about significant improvements in the organization's competitiveness over a longer period of time, usually 3-5 years. But a big difference should be the audacity of their respective objectives. In this day and age competitive strategies need to be built on breakthroughs, not business-as-usual plus 10%.

The most pivotal part of building the Strategy-on-a-Page is to establish the critical few breakthrough objectives that if delivered will fulfill your strategic intent. This is no trivial task since once established the organization will be committing substantial resources (time, money, people) towards these objectives.

First, it should be recalled that these are breakthrough objectives, not business-as-usual goals. A vision of a different tomorrow is rarely achieved in small, incremental steps (10% performance increases year on year), but can be achieved with bold leaps in performance, which almost always necessitates changing the way we do things. Too often we want a better future but continue to work on incremental objectives in risk-averse ways.

> *The definition of insanity is doing the same thing*
> *over and over again and expecting different results.*
> *~ Albert Einstein*

Breakthrough Objectives have the added benefit of requiring innovative thinking and cross-functional approaches in order to be achieved. Equally important is that Breakthrough Objectives should help build significant capability inside the company that didn't exist before. Achieving significant financial results via cost cutting alone is really no breakthrough at all, since there is little attention paid to capability building.

A Breakthrough 'Mindset'

At the limits of performance, the difference between winning and losing is not just about physical and mental strength, but about changing the rules and adopting a different strategy. ~ Alistair Schofield

In the 2006 British Open golf tournament at the beautiful Royal Liverpool Golf Club at Hoylake, Tiger Woods, Ernie Ells and Chris DiMarco all played brilliantly but Tiger Woods won by adopting a radically different strategy to everyone else; not using a driver to tee off on the longer holes.

Although this strategy caused consternation amongst many golf commentators, the result was that he not only won by two strokes but also set a course record for the lowest total score during an Open championship, beating the previous record by eight strokes.

While most players are busy building on conventional wisdom to perfect their game, it takes real bravery to challenge the established processes and adopt a different strategy. But breakthrough results are nearly always a result of breakthrough thinking.

Another great example of breakthrough thinking is the story of Roger Bannister running the first sub-4-minute mile. For many years it was widely believed to be physically impossible for a human to run a mile (1609 meters) in under four minutes. In fact, until Bannister achieved it in 1954, many believed the four-minute mile to be a physical barrier that no man could break, in much the same way as pilots had once regarded the sound barrier.

Bannister, a medical student, could not see any particular physical reason why such a barrier should exist. After all, a mile is simply an arbitrary measure of distance and he knew he could run a quarter mile in under one minute, so why not just do that four times in a row?

Having convinced himself that a physical barrier did not exist, Bannister ran a mile in 3 minutes 59.4 seconds on 6th May 1954. Interestingly, John Lander, another runner from that era, also ran a mile in under 4 minutes just 56 days later and, by the end of 1957, no less than 16 other athletes had achieved the same feat, proving that a physiological barrier had not existed, but a mental barrier had!

The same is true with many businesses, which all too frequently limit their thinking to what is reasonable rather than what is desired. In the 1950s Toyota took a giant step forward from the normal production-line environment and gave power to front-line employees, having workers cooperate in working groups to raise quality and productivity. For decades the early adopters of Lean Production Techniques significantly outperformed the big US automakers on quality and speed of vehicle delivery.

The average strategic plan is a perfect example of "bounded thinking". In most companies the starting point is usually the previous plan. It is therefore no surprise that the new plan invariably ends up looking like the previous plan, plus a bit extra. But it was not this sort of incremental thinking that led Nokia to abandon its roots as a lumbering and tire manufacturing company to become one of the world leaders in mobile phones, nor persuaded Apple to break into the music entertainment industry with the launch of the iPod and iTunes. These were breakthrough strategies.

So, you are probably thinking; *"Okay, but how do we develop breakthrough objectives that are significantly stretch for us but not so huge that they become impossible to achieve and thus demoralizing for everybody and ruinous for the company?"*

Think like a New Entrant

We cannot solve our problems with the same thinking used when we created them. ~ Albert Einstein

One very useful approach is to think of yourself from the perspective of a new entrant into your marketplace. New entrants have no bond with the status quo. A new entrant cannot expect to succeed in the marketplace by using structures, practices and processes like those used by incumbents. To be successful the new entrant must aim well beyond existing market standards. They must devise offerings and practices that will deliver substantially superior products and/or performance. It is this *'mindset'* that you should adopt to think about your own Breakthrough Objectives.

Embracing the *'new entrant mindset'* can allow the senior team to approach the development of Breakthrough Objectives without the legacy thinking that typically keeps incumbents from making dramatic improvements.

To begin, you should ask yourselves these types of questions:

What do customers really want?
- Virgin has made big inroads into several industries by realizing that customers want to be treated like people, not a number, and have some fun along the way.

- Ryan Air and Easy Jet have taken a big chunk of market share in Europe by understanding that there is a large section of the population that want very low fares and will put up with no frills, especially for their holiday travel.

What kind of workplace policies and practices would create loyal and engaged employees?

- Continental threw away the dreaded 'policy manual' and told counter agents to use their best judgment to help the customer without unduly hurting the company – customer satisfaction soared, as did profitability.
- Google makes working long hours fun with numerous workplace amenities like free haircuts, fitness equipment, laundry facilities and on-site medical staff

What would be a revolutionary product or service that would shake up this marketplace?

- Recall the impact of the mass-produced automobile, the helicopter, the Sony Walkman or the Apple iPod?

What ideas or technologies could we adopt from other industries to give us a big advantage?

- Amazon created the virtual bookstore by applying Internet technology to retail book sales.
- Continental's adoption of a decision support algorithm from software company CALEB generated near-optimal crew recovery solutions in a matter of minutes after a major schedule disruption due to weather, thus saving the airline millions.

Chapter 17:
STRATEGY AS A BALANCING ACT

Balance is the key to power. ~ Thomas D. Willhite

When the average executive thinks about business objectives, 80% of the time a set of financial numbers and P&L figures come to mind. We now know that financial success is only a part of the overall ability of a company to have a healthy, sustainable future. Today's Investment Banking debacle is a great example. Big banks earn billions but the future of the entire banking enterprise is in jeopardy due to other issues: greed culture, insider trading, unsustainable products like derivatives, poor customer service, excessive staff turnover, etc.

In a 1992 Harvard Business Review article [28] entitled *The Balanced Scorecard - Measures that Drive Performance,* Robert S. Kaplan and David P. Norton made popular the term *'Balanced Scorecard'* to show that other factors besides financial were critical to sustainable business performance.

The early Balanced Scorecards comprised simple tables broken into four sections. Typically these perspectives were labeled Financial, Customer, Internal Business Processes, and Learning & Growth. Completing the Balanced Scorecard then required selecting five or six good measures (metrics) for each perspective. The Strategy-on-a-Page Execution Roadmap uses a similar balanced format for the Breakthrough Objectives but is focused on strategic rather than operational elements.

There are various ways of looking at your organization's Breakthrough Objectives in a balanced format. For example, Continental Airlines chose to focus on four Breakthrough Objectives categories:

- People
- Product
- Marketplace
- Financial

One of our clients in the defense sector used five categories of Breakthrough Objectives:

- People
- Product
- Operations
- Marketplace
- Financial

Toyota's True North metrics cover all aspects of improvement and impact all the key lines on income statements and balance sheets, while focusing on only four key metric areas. The Toyota four key areas are:

- Human Development: Toyota's commitment to people

development is seen in their ubiquitous phrase: "We build people before we build cars."

- Quality
- Cycle Time (time it takes from order to delivery is one of their key focuses)
- Cost/Productivity

And many clients tend to focus on all or some of the following Breakthrough Categories because they tend to better represent cross-functional objectives in which nearly every function or department can participate:

- People
- Quality
- Product
- Safety
- Customer
- Costs

Our recommendation is to use Breakthrough Categories that don't easily fit into functional or departmental segments. Using cross-functional and organization-wide categories helps break down the silo-focus and foster more *'enterprise thinking.'*

In order to bring these strategy perspectives to life for the organization it is often useful to develop a short descriptive *'theme'* for each. In the Continental Airlines turnaround they chose the following themes for each of their four breakthrough categories:

People:	Working Together
Product:	Make Reliability a Reality
Marketplace:	Fly to Win
Financial:	Fund the Future

In the words of Gordon Bethune, CEO of Continental Airlines and architect of the turnaround:

> *"Don't use fancy words to make things sound better than they are or try to impress people. Build your breakthrough objectives using straight, clear, everyday language that your employees will understand."*

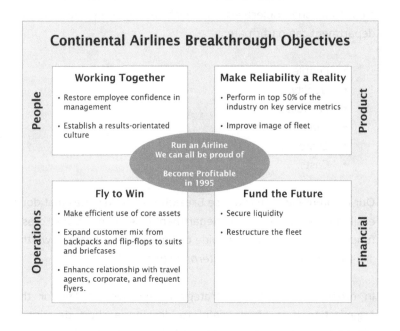

Our recommendation is that each category have anywhere from 1-2, sometimes 3, high level Breakthrough Objectives that describe a specific end-state scenario. At this point, don't worry about the metrics or the numbers; what is needed here is a clear '*mental picture*' of the end result.

For example, one of the early Ford strategy documents in 2007 spells out their set of balanced breakthrough objectives (with the overall Strategic Intent in the center):

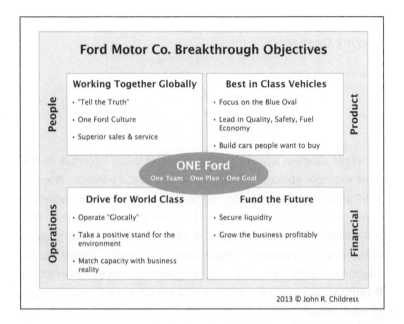

Again, these are high-level, directional Breakthrough Objectives. Each paints a clear picture of the end result and is in plain language that everyone can understand, not management-speak or academic obfuscation. A great rule of thumb when creating your Breakthrough Objectives is *'tell it like it is'* and point to the future!

For example, the Ford People Breakthrough Objective *"Tell the Truth"* refers to the previous Ford culture where information and presentations were sanitized as they went further and further up the corporate ladder. The old culture of *'don't bring me no bad news'* had to be changed in order for Ford to effectively deliver on its turnaround strategy.

The acid test for a good set of Key Breakthrough Objectives is whether employees at all levels can easily understand what you want to achieve.

Digging Deeper

We shall not cease from exploration, and the end of all our exploring will be to arrive where we started and know the place for the first time. ~ T. S. Eliot

Let's take a look at what is behind a Breakthrough Objective. In the Ford example above, the statement, *"Build Cars People Want to Buy"*, gives a good indication of the desired objective. However, in order to drive the development of funded strategic initiatives that will deliver the breakthroughs, a more comprehensive scoping document is required. Hyperlinked to each Breakthrough Objective item in the **Strategy-on-a-Page Execution Roadmap** is a scoping template that contains the following types of information:

- Brief description of this objective
- Breakthrough required
- Outcome(s) desired
- Potential value to be delivered
- Why this is a breakthrough
- Potential barriers to realizing this breakthrough
- Additional business benefits expected
- Risks associated with non-delivery
- (you can add additional information as you feel necessary)

The value of the Breakthrough Objective Scoping Document is that anyone in the business, after reading, should have a good understanding of why this breakthrough is important to the future of the organization. A complete scoping template also gives guidance to those who will be accountable for developing strategic initiatives and projects intended to deliver the breakthrough.

Breakthrough Objective Scoping Document

Breakthrough Objective: _____

Category: _____ Theme: _____

Why this is a breakthrough	Brief description of this objective
Potential barriers	Breakthrough required
Additional business benefits expected	Outcome desired
Risks associated with non-delivery	Potential value to be delivered

2013 © John R. Childress

Chapter 18:

STRATEGIC INITIATIVES – WHERE THE RUBBER MEETS THE ROAD

Success seems to be connected with action. Successful
people keep moving. They make mistakes, learn along the
way, and keep moving. ~ Conrad Hilton

We now come to the fun part of the **Strategy-on-a-Page Execution Roadmap** development – the *'action items'*, or as we call them, *'Strategic Initiatives'* and *'Projects.'* Strategic Initiatives represent the most significant business projects and link directly to the Breakthrough Objectives. Strategic Initiatives are critical to the overall delivery of the business strategy and help:

- bring discipline and rigor to planning and execution
- ensure that the timing and achievement of milestones and deliverables are agreed upon and managed
- tie investment of CAPEX and OPEX to specific and measurable outcomes
- enable issues to be addressed and resolved proactively, before they jeopardize outcomes

Successful Strategic Initiatives have a number of key characteristics:

- Few, Not Many – we suggest no more than 3-4 for each Breakthrough Objective (the *'right'* number often depends on organizational maturity and purpose)

- Strategic Impact – directly linked to a specific Breakthrough Objective

- 6 – 15 month duration

- Formally documented using a standard scoping template (Strategic Initiative Scoping worksheet)

- An individual senior executive is directly accountable and recruits a cross-functional project team

- Reported on and discussed by the senior leadership team during the regular Strategy Review Meetings

- Each Strategic Initiative has a business case, ROI, and resources (Capital or Operating $$, FTE, etc.) allocated to its successful delivery.

One of the problems when trying to develop Strategic Initiatives is the belief that they have to be *'perfectly developed'* before we can commit resources to them. There is no such thing as a perfect project (or a perfect project plan for that matter)! The process of achieving the desired results from a plan is more heuristic than stochastic – which is a fancy way of saying that a good plan put into action will give us feedback along the way that can be used to improve the plan in real time. We can't think of everything in the planning stage, but we can respond along the way to things that come up in order to continuously improve the plan and therefore improve the probability of a successful outcome.

The best way to approach the development of strategic initiatives is to set aside the initiatives and projects already underway and start fresh by taking each Breakthrough Objective and asking the question:

"What one initiative (project), if well-funded, staffed and executed, would (with a high degree of certainty) deliver this specific Breakthrough Objective?"

It is suggested that everyone independently come up with one initiative for each Breakthrough Objective, which they feel most strongly would deliver the business benefits, then look at all the initiatives together. In most cases two things become apparent:

- One initiative tends to appear most frequently.
- Usually there is a cluster of 3-4 that dominate the list

These are your best candidates for inclusion onto the **Strategy-on-a-Page Execution Roadmap**. But the most important point is to have an active debate with the entire team about which initiatives will best guarantee the delivery of the Breakthrough Objectives. At this point it is also imperative to bring in the current initiatives, if there are any that people are working on already, to check and make certain they should be continued or discontinued, according to whether or not they will help deliver the Breakthrough Objectives.

Here is an example of two strategic initiatives linked to one Breakthrough Objective.

A Project Plan and Business Case for Each Strategic Initiative

A critical ingredient for effective governance and delivery of the overall strategic plan is to develop *'high level'* project plans for each Strategic Initiative. By having a project plan for each initiative regular governance is more effective through the use of plan-to-actual tracking dashboards, detailed project actions with appropriate accountability at each step, plus the opportunity for appropriate countermeasures when the results are falling behind plan.

It is the role of the initiative owner and the project team to develop an Initiative Scoping document and then a robust Initiative Project Plan. Within the **Strategy-on-a-Page Execution Roadmap** templates can be imbedded and accessed by activating the appropriate cell within the list of strategic initiatives.

The Initiative Scoping Document should contain the following minimum elements:

- Initiative Owner: Name, email and phone number
- Initiative Title
- Brief Description of the Initiative
- End-state Objective
- Intended Benefits
- Perceived Obstacles
- Initial Understanding of Root Cause
- Scope (what is in scope and what is not)
- Deliverables Expected
- Project Team (names, phone number, emails)
- Business Case (ROI and Cost-Benefit assessment of the project)
- Resource requirements

This document is essential in assisting the team in developing a comprehensive action plan for the specific strategic initiatives.

Also attached to the **Strategy-on-a-Page Execution Roadmap**, hyperlinked to the Strategic Initiative buttons, are the Strategic Initiative Planning Template and Strategic Initiative Countermeasures documents. These documents contain the following information that the team uses to deliver on their plan and report progress at the regular Strategy Review Meetings.

- Step-by-Step action plans for implementation of the initiative with due dates and assigned accountability
- Regular (usually monthly or every two weeks) milestones
- Tracking for Plan-to-Actual results by month
- Appropriate countermeasures when required.

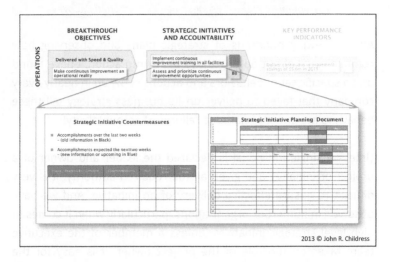

2013 © John R. Childress

Close Enough for Horseshoes and Hand Grenades

There is no perfect plan, but the sooner you begin to work your plan, the sooner you learn how to improve your plan.

Most organizations make the mistake of striving for an excellent, even a perfect, project plan, mostly on the false belief that there is such a thing, and partly because of the erroneous belief that the more analysis the better the plan. Both assumptions are false when it comes to strategic initiatives, and strategies in general. At best a strategic plan is a directionally correct estimate at a given period of time.

My recommendation is to build your strategic initiative plans at about an 80% confidence level, then get started and learn as you go, using recently acquired experience-based knowledge to improve and refine the plan.

If Everyone is Accountable, No One is Accountable

Accountability breeds response-ability. ~ Stephen R. Covey

After reviewing hundreds of strategic plans and observing how companies go about putting those plans into action, I have found that a specific set of behaviors and actions show up in nearly every company that failed to deliver on its business strategy. All these behaviors are directly related to failures of accountability!

Unless a single individual is declared the leader and owner of a project or initiative and given all the required authority, it is very difficult to ensure effective delivery of an initiative. And we have observed in numerous organizations, particularly when it comes to high level strategic initiatives, unless a member of the executive team takes on the role of the project owner, it is easy for the project to get stalled because of the need for senior approval when real business change and hard decisions are required.

And by *'owner'* we are not referring to executive sponsor; that is someone who just acts as a liaison for the project team and doesn't really accept full accountability for the performance of the team. In most cases executive sponsors are a waste of time, they fail to get fully engaged, believing instead that they should be a communication conduit rather than fully accountable. Unless the project is owned by a member of the senior executive team, who accepts the full performance accountability, there is little chance that barriers to the success of the project can be successfully navigated or changed.

The role of the executive owner (accountable owner) is to define the requirements, recruit a team to work the project, and to accept the full accountability for the successful delivery of that particular initiative. There is a Strategic Initiative Accountability template worksheet for each initiative describing the personal commitment of the executive owner.

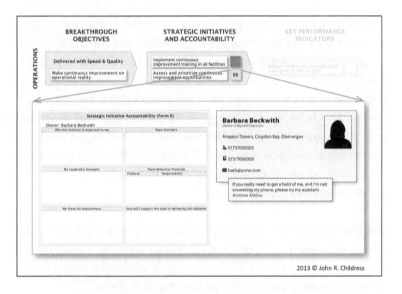

And experience has shown that the executive owner who recruits a cross-functional project team is able to come up with better innovative solutions to problems confronting the successful delivery of initiatives. Another benefit of having individual members of the senior team accept the accountability for strategic initiatives outside their normal function is the fact that it forces them to think outside their silo and to become more knowledgeable about the entire business. In the words of one CEO:

> *Having members of my senior team head up*
> *strategic initiatives outside their normal*
> *functional role has given them a broader set of*
> *experiences. They have gained an invaluable*
> *CEO-perspective.*

Making it Personal

> *Yes, Officer. I did see the speed limit sign.*
> *I just didn't see you!*

I've been reading about the impact of traffic signs that show motorists their speed. These are often put up in residential areas or construction zones. The purpose is to give real-time feedback to the driver about how fast he/she is going. And it seems to work. I know that when I am driving I have, like many others, the tendency to drive and think of other things at the same time. Not the best approach to safe driving, but very natural for all of us. So when a motorist sees a digital sign that displays his/her actual speed, it helps them to switch off autopilot, check their speedometer and pay more attention to safe driving.

And the statistics are favorable. According to one study 75% of drivers who see their individual car speed flashing, immediately slow down and are more cautious, staying within the speed limit for approximately 5 miles after passing the digital sign. [29]

To me, this is a great example of the power of 'personalizing data'; that is making it about me, and not just otherwise impersonal information. For example, a printed speed sign, say 35 mph, is impersonal and really doesn't get much attention in this fast-moving, data overload world we live in. But a flashing digital speed sign that specifically focuses on my speed becomes personalized data and, as the study shows, the impact lasts for miles after the event.

So, what's this got to do with Strategic Initiatives? Quite a lot, actually. One of the reasons most strategies fail is that the information given out at most meetings, like current revenue, current forecast, current EBITDA, sales funnel numbers, customer service scores, etc. is useful, but impersonal. They are collective numbers and collectively we are supposed to do something about them, either reverse a negative trend or keep a positive trend going.

In these types of meetings or business reviews, everyone nods their heads, makes notes, promises to do better, then it's back to business as usual. The data wasn't personal and so the strategy lumbers along, often sidelined by daily 'firefighting' and immediate problem solving.

Every seasoned executive knows that if everyone is accountable, nobody's accountable!

The **Strategy-on-a-Page Execution Roadmap**, however, has built-in personalized data. Strategic Initiatives have specific individual owners who are fully accountable to the entire organization for the delivery of an important piece of the strategic plan. And each member of the senior leadership team is personally accountable for one or more strategic initiatives. And when your project data is shown during the strategy review meetings, in front of all the other executives, this data suddenly becomes very personal.

Peer pressure to perform well, not let the team down, to 'look good' to the boss, and all the other human factors associated with personal motivation now come strongly into focus. Personalized data helps you and I take the situation more seriously and the impact in terms of correction actions, countermeasures, and improved results is focused and substantial.

Most people say:

>*"Don't take it personal, it's just business!"*

But I say:

>*"Take it personal. It's about leadership!"*

Chapter 19:
KILL ALL THE PETS!

Winning teams have the least amount of distractions.
They have a really tight group of people working
towards the same common goal. ~ Larry Dixon

Every time I conduct senior executive interviews prior to a strategy execution consulting engagement I hear complaints about *'Initiative Overload'*. More often than not a bleary-eyed executive looks at me, shakes her head, and says something like:

> *"I know you are trying to help, but the last thing I need right now is another initiative. If you really want to help this company, reduce the number of projects! There's no way we can get all our current projects done, even with twice the staff."*

Sound familiar? Initiative Overload is a common problem in nearly every company. Somehow initiatives behave like rabbits, they seem to multiply and grow, all with good intentions on the part of their sponsors. *"We need this project to be funded if we are going to remain competitive. My department can't deliver on its objectives unless we invest in this new technology."* The rationale is totally logical and it's hard to say no; after all, the senior executive is fully supportive.

So how do otherwise rational and logical senior executive teams wind up in a situation of initiative overload? Where do these added projects, and increased costs come from? And why do otherwise powerful senior executives feel so frustrated and helpless in solving this problem?

The answer lies in the fact that most companies are silo-based in how they execute their strategy. While the overall strategy has an enterprise-wide focus, implementation plans are usually developed by each department, acting in isolation. Each department or function develops the plans and initiatives they believe will best deliver the strategy, but from their own functional, or silo, point of view. In addition, a few pet projects are also added to the mix, mostly because a senior department head thinks it's a good idea. The result: initiative overload and cost inflation.

Whenever we have audited the number of active projects inside a company against the specific strategic objectives of the firm, more often than not we find a large number, close to 30% which are not directly linked to the overall strategic objectives of the company.

Most CEOs are shocked when this situation is brought to light. *"How did these things get funded?"* is often the cry from the corner office. It also creates an uproar from the sponsors of those projects deemed *'not connected.'*

And here is where leadership and teamwork must come into play. Those projects and initiatives that don't connect to the overall strategic intent or help deliver the Breakthrough Objectives need to be cut (unless of course you are one of the few companies with an unlimited budget and an endless supply of good people).

Here are the key questions the senior team must address, collectively, in order to reduce the number of initiatives:

- Just how does this initiative directly connect to our strategic intent and our breakthrough objectives?
- What would happen 3-5 years from now if this project were cut today?
- Where could we better deploy the cash and human resources currently consumed by this project?

Let's assume you only have 15% of all projects and initiatives that are not connected to your overall strategy. Where could you better deploy 15% of your budget and people?

Initiative Overload is a problem worth tackling.

Chapter 20:
KPIs – WHAT GETS MEASURED GETS DELIVERED

What's measured improves. ~ Peter Drucker

Breakthrough Objectives are by definition high level, qualitative pictures of a set of desired end-states that will drive the business forward to fulfilling its Strategic Intent. However, unless we put specific metrics and milestones onto these objectives, they will become difficult to track and manage, nor can we accurately know on a real-time basis whether our efforts are producing results, or how far off track we may be.

Our philosophy on the importance of metrics in strategy execution can be summarized in the following quotes:

- *"If you don't keep score, you are only practicing."*
- *"A strategy without metrics is just a wish. And metrics that are not aligned with strategic objectives are a waste of time."*

- *"Be careful what you measure—you might just get it."* That is, by measuring something, you are declaring to your managers and employees that an activity is important.

Clear, concise and relevant metrics serve multiple purposes within the strategy execution process:

- **Governance**: Metrics allow us to manage and govern the overall focus, attention and resources we give to certain business activities.

- **Reporting**: This is the most commonly identified function of metrics. We use the Strategy-on-a-Page metrics to report performance to ourselves, our employees and sometimes even the Board of Directors.

- **Communication**: This is a critical but often overlooked function of a metric. We use metrics to tell people both internally and externally what constitutes value and what the key success factors are. People can't easily see value, but they readily understand metrics.

- **Opportunities for Improvement**: Metrics identify gaps between performance and the expectation. Intervention takes place when we have to close undesired gaps. The size of the gap, the nature of the gap, whether it is positive or negative, and the importance of the activity determine the need for management to resolve these gaps.

- **Expectations**: Metrics frame expectations both internally (with your staff) and externally (with your customers). Metrics help form what the customer expects. For example, if we say that we deliver by 9:30 a.m. next day, we have formed both a metric (i.e., did we meet the 9:30 a.m. deadline) and an expectation. We will satisfy our customer if the order arrives by 9:30 a.m. We will disappoint otherwise.

Understanding Key Performance Indicators (KPIs)

The first important insight into establishing and using KPIs is to understand the difference between a KPI and an Enterprise Metric. Enterprise Metrics are the real numbers about how well an organization is performing as an enterprise. These are normally profit and loss numbers and also those key metrics found on the balance sheet. The most common enterprise metrics are Revenue, Profit, and Cash. These are real numbers, the kind you go to the bank with.

KPIs are what we call *'directional metrics'* or *'directional indicators'* and give you directional feedback in various areas.

KPIs should be used primarily for learning and making improvement decisions. An appropriate KPI will provide the required information to assist in navigating towards the desired results. Within the Strategy-on-a-Page Execution Roadmap, KPIs are the metrics used to determine if the organization is making progress on delivering on the promises of the Breakthrough Objectives.

Again, the important distinction to understand is that the KPIs on the **Strategy-on-a-Page Execution Roadmap** are performance indicators and not enterprise results metrics such as profitability, revenue, and cash generation.

For example, if the Breakthrough Objective is *"Create and Support a One Team Culture"*, then there may be several Strategic Initiatives (defined projects) put in place to fulfill the Breakthrough Objective, and one (or more) KPIs to measure progress.

In the example above, the KPI linked to the People Breakthrough Objective is a Pulse Survey score. In this case the Pulse Survey is comprised of 20 questions that, in total, describe the new culture desired. By implementing the Pulse Survey to sample groups of employees each month, an average score (metric) can be developed. In this case, with a range of available scores between 1 and 10, this organization uses an average score of >7.0 as the baseline for achieving a One Team Culture.

The KPI then can be reviewed on a regular basis, in this case monthly following the distribution of the Pulse Survey, as to whether or not the organization is making progress on the Breakthrough Objective of *"Create and Support a One Team Culture."* To display the current progress of this KPI metric, all that is required is to activate the KPI cell in the **Strategy-on-a-Page Execution Roadmap**.

As shown, over the past 9 months of Pulse Surveys, the average score has improved to above the Pulse Survey Baseline of 7.00, indicating the promise of the Breakthrough Objective ("Create and Support a One Team Culture") is being delivered by the various Strategic Initiatives put in place.

A second example, dealing with a Breakthrough Objective, this time in the Operations area *("Make Continuous Improvement an Operational Reality")*, culminates in a clear KPI metric *("Deliver Continuous Improvement Savings of $5.6m in 2013")*. Again, clicking on the KPI button reveals the current progress against plan for this metric.

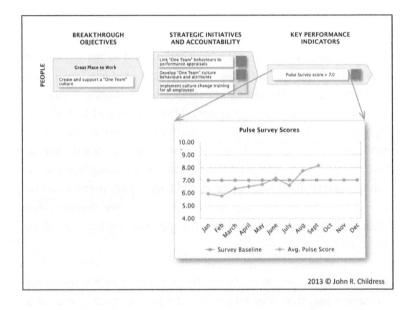

2013 © John R. Childress

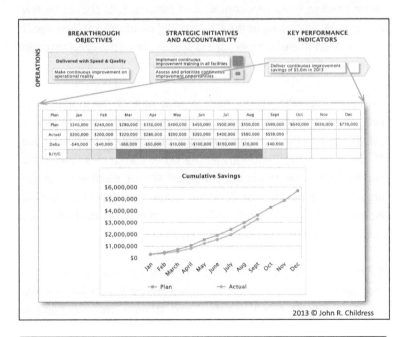

2013 © John R. Childress

Healers or Coroners? - Leading and Lagging KPIs

An autopsy helps all those concerned (doctors, police, family members), except of course, the deceased.

There are two major types of KPIs: 'Leading' and 'Lagging.' Leading indicators measure activities that give a preview to future performance and upcoming challenges, while lagging indicators measure the output of past activity. Most financial KPIs deal with lagging metrics, while some KPIs, such as number of sales calls scheduled for the next three months, give a forward look at upcoming activities and would be considered a leading indicator of future performance. Both Leading and Lagging KPI metrics can be useful for effective strategy execution if they give management useful information to make changes that will impact the future outcome.

One important thing to watch out for concerning KPIs is that most managers feel that they should get the perfect metric, and as a result, tend to build very complicated metrics. KPIs should be few and simple. By looking at the KPI it should be obvious to just about anyone what these numbers are telling us about the Breakthrough Objective.

At one of our clients, we noticed that one of the nurses was keeping track of the number of Band-Aids used during the week. It was curious to her that this particular organization tended to use 10 times as many Band-Aids as the other companies where she had worked. While this is not a *'normal'* KPI, we discovered, at the urging of the nurse, that Band-Aid usage was a perfect leading indicator for unsafe work practices, which if unchecked could eventually lead to a lost work-time accident.

By noticing the trend in Band-Aid usage it was possible for management to discover potential unsafe work (lack of training, unsafe standards, poorly designed work stations, etc.) areas and to improve the process before any major accident. KPIs, if properly constructed, will help you improve your organization's performance by acting as early warning signals. Remember, it's the trend that is important, not the absolute number of Band-Aids, or any other number.

To learn more about KPIs and how best to use them, we suggest a very comprehensive book by David Palmenter; *Key Performance Indicators: Developing, Implementing, and Using Winning KPIs.* *(Palmenter 2010)*

Chapter 21:
THE PRIZE – ENTERPRISE METRICS

Press forward. Do not stop, do not linger in your journey,
but strive for the mark set before you. ~ George Whitefield

The ultimate purpose of a well-crafted and executed strategy is to improve the overall fortunes of your organization. The **Strategy-on-a-Page Execution Roadmap** lays out the entire journey, from Strategic Drivers to Enterprise Metrics, which allow the senior team to lead the process of effective strategy execution.

The actions and investments in strategic initiatives and other activities should move the needle on the important *'Enterprise Metrics.'* Each organization tends to define their ultimate Enterprise Metrics differently, putting more emphasis on some and less on others. In general, we have found at least three major financial Enterprise Metrics in nearly every company:

- Revenue (Actual vs. Plan)
- Net Profit or EBIT (Actual vs. Plan)
- Cash (Actual vs. Plan)

Occasionally, organizations focus on additional financial metrics that are important in their business, such as:

- Total Backlog ($$)
- ROIC (Return on Invested Capital)
- R&D Invested (% of total revenue)
- Revenue per Employee

Some organizations also use non-financial enterprise metrics that are critical in their industry such as:

- Employee Satisfaction Index
- Customer Satisfaction Score
- Others?

Enterprise Metrics are usually measured on a monthly basis, and if properly crafted, can also give a forward look at expected performance as well as current month information. In this example, the KPI shows not only plan vs. actual cash position for each month, but also a 3-month forward estimate, providing both Lagging and Leading indicators.

Enterprise Metric: Cash (Plan vs Actual)

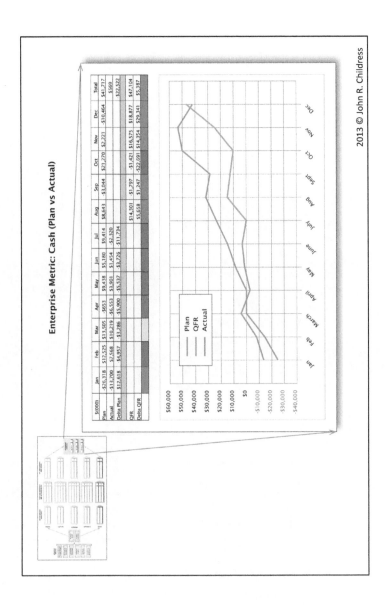

$(000)	Jan	Feb	Mar	Apr	May	Jun	Jul	Aug	Sep	Oct	Nov	Dec	Total
Plan	-$26,318	$12,525	$13,505	-$653	$9,438	$5,180	$9,414	$8,643	-$3,044	$21,270	$2,221	$10,464	$41,717
Actual	-$13,700	$7,568	$10,219	-$6,553	$3,901	$1,454	-$2,320						$569
Delta Plan	$12,618	$4,957	$13,286	-$5,900	$5,537	$3,726	-$11,734						$22,522
QFR								$14,301	-$1,797	-$1,421	$16,575	$18,877	$47,104
Delta_QFR								$5,658	$1,247	-$22,691	$14,354	$29,341	$5,387

Legend: Plan, QFR, Actual

$60,000
$50,000
$40,000
$30,000
$20,000
$10,000
$0
-$10,000
-$20,000
-$30,000
-$40,000

Jan Feb March April May June July Aug Sept Oct Nov Dec

SECTION FOUR:
HANGING TOGETHER OR HANGING TOGETHER

We must all hang together or assuredly we shall all hang separately. ~ Benjamin Franklin

What makes the **FASTBREAK Strategy Execution** process uniquely effective is the additional focus on Leadership, Team Dynamics and Culture Change, in addition to the Performance Management and dashboard elements. While the performance management tools and the **Strategy-on-a-Page Execution Roadmap** are robust methodologies, without aligned leadership and a supportive culture, it is difficult to effectively execute.

A good analogy is a high performance automobile. The aerodynamics are right, the car has a performance engine and all the latest technology, but without aligned tires (an aligned leadership team) and without gasoline (a supportive corporate culture), it looks great but goes nowhere.

In the next two chapters we will focus on Leadership Alignment and Corporate Culture, the invisible ingredients, in order to better understand why most strategies wind up poorly executed and what you, the CEO, can do to get all the elements working together.

Chapter 22:
STRATEGIC LEADERSHIP AND ALIGNMENT

*That which is to be most desired in [a team] is oneness and
not sameness. Sameness is the worst thing that could
happen to [a team]. To make all people the same would
lower their quality, but oneness would raise it.*
~ Stephen S. Wise

Imagine this modern twist on the old story of Rip van Winkle.

The very weird day of 'Kip' van Winkle, senior executive:

*It took Kip most of breakfast to fully wake up. After all, 50 years
asleep is a rather long time, but he didn't know that yet. The
last he could remember was tossing and turning in bed after a
particularly stressful day at the office – committee meetings,
customer problems, cheap imports flooding the market. He
recalled taking a couple of sleeping tablets and now felt
unusually groggy.*

Showered, shaved and dressed, his mind was on the coming business day as he took the subway to work. Looking around, something didn't seem quite right – things looked and felt different, but sleepy commuters were still going to work, just as always, so he thought nothing of it – must still be the lingering effects of the sleeping tablets. The elevators were the same, so he felt a sense of relief as he crowded in with the others. It was when the doors opened onto the executive floor of ACME Industries that he realized something was terribly wrong! This was definitely not his sleepy old company.

Everywhere people were running about in what seemed like a frantic pace. Was there a disaster or something, he wondered? The staff at ACME never moved this fast, not even when the big boss called. And many of them were talking into strange looking miniature devices held up to one ear – and the weird ringing sounds – what happened to the familiar Ma Bell ring tone? He paused at the desk of one of the secretaries and noticed a most bizarre looking typewriter – she was typing words onto a miniature television screen, not on paper. And he couldn't see any carbons. He stood and watched as one of the executive assistants stared into her little screen and flipped through what looked like a vast library with just a few keystrokes. Access to unlimited information at the touch of a button! What the hell was going on?

Everywhere Kip turned he felt out of place – strange, unable to comprehend the changes that had overcome his workplace – the speed of activity, information access, and instant communications while you move about. Completely disoriented, he moved towards the boardroom, realizing it was time for the senior staff meeting, his head still buzzing.

The meeting was already underway. He paused, looked around, listened for a moment, and felt instantly at ease. Everything was the same – at least things hadn't changed at the top!

Rethinking the Role of the Senior Team

The main ingredient of stardom is the rest of the team.
~ John Wooden

Ever since the publication of *In Search of Excellence* in 1982 a growing tidal wave of business improvement tools and techniques have helped businesses around the globe become more productive. Such tools and techniques as reengineering, EVA, design-to-manufacture, six sigma, lean, balanced scorecard, supply-chain integration, strategic outsourcing and other tools have reduced costs, improved productivity and helped capture market share. In addition, advances in technology (email, video-conferencing, personal computing, and, of course, the Internet) have dramatically improved the speed and velocity of business. Together these advances have dramatically changed the lives and work practices of nearly every group and function inside a company. Except one – the senior leadership team.

This group, unarguably the most influential in the company, has remained largely outside the focus and pressure of process improvement. Their work practices remain much the same as they were 50 (or more) years ago (aside from email, teleconferencing and other technology related speed enablers – and we now know that speed, without redesigning work processes can lead to reduced efficiency, increased stress and even process breakdown). Not only are the work practices and processes of the senior team largely unchanged, in most companies they are largely unmapped, undefined and poorly standardized. In addition, the senior leadership team is usually seen, by themselves and others, as immune from any business improvement process.

Traditionally the senior team and its work has been seen as separate, outside of, and removed from, the fundamental work processes that go on inside the business.

I take the opposite view. The work and behavior of the senior leadership team has a dramatic impact on overall company performance in numerous ways and when they chose not to use process improvement tools on their own collective activities, the work of the senior team can actually destroy economic value through redundant, inefficient and time consuming activities (think about meetings or the time spent by middle management getting ready for a review with senior management). Non value-add activities are known as waste. And waste at the top tends to have a magnifying effect on those below.

Leadership studies in the past have mostly focused on behavioral characteristics, ultimately leading to the current *cult of charisma* and *quick fixes* now rampant in a plethora of popular business books and in the press. However, in today's difficult global economic environment, organizational efficiency and business effectiveness are again taking center stage. Not since the controversial article by Abraham Zaleznik on the real work of leadership [30] and the writings of Jon Katzenbach and Douglas Smith on senior teams [31] [32] have we paused to ask some fundamental questions of those at the top of the business.

- What is the real work of the senior team?
- How do they create value?
- In what ways can they actually destroy value (without knowing it)?
- How can the senior team be more productive and ensure greater business success?
- Is there a better way to organize and lead?

In the past, these questions have gone unasked and unanswered, largely due to the overall robustness of a growing global economy fuelled by easy access to capital. After all, leadership must have been doing its job as evidenced by rising share prices and record bonuses. But today, with a global recession still struggling to recover, companies are facing unprecedented challenges that threaten their very survival.

Risk is everywhere, aggregate demand is collapsing, funding at all levels is difficult or impossible to obtain, competition is becoming cut-throat, morale is low and key employees are vulnerable. Executives and senior teams, for the most part, have little experience navigating such perilous waters. However, strategic opportunities abound for those who, instead of automatically defaulting to cost cutting and layoffs, are willing to rethink the work of leadership.

What if we looked at the work of the senior team as a set of *'business processes'*? First of all, what is the work of the senior team? What are their real outputs? What if we used process improvement techniques, like lean sigma, 5S, visual metrics, and feedback loops to improve the work of the senior team?

The Work of Leadership isn't Working

Insanity is doing the same thing over and over and expecting different results. ~ Albert Einstein

When the dust settles on the recent meltdown of the global financial markets much of the fault will be attributed to poor leadership – especially at the top of large financial institutions where leaders were unable to stem personal and corporate greed. The fault also lies in regulatory bodies unwilling to impose the requisite oversight and accountability required for the stewardship of billions of dollars of other people's money.

Further evidence for the failure of leadership lies in the fact that with several decades of economic prosperity we have witnessed a steady and dramatic decline in employee engagement and a growing lack of trust in leadership, not just inside companies, but in nearly all our global institutions. Today people see the future, both their own personal future and the economic and political state of the world, with growing pessimism, concern and in many cases, fear. And when people feel uncertain about their leaders and the future, productivity suffers.

But how can this be? Leadership training and MBA degrees are more popular than ever. Executive Leadership courses at major business schools are oversubscribed. Mega leadership conferences like the *World Business Forum*, billed as a two-day transformational experience for leaders looking to achieve results, draws thousands of executives to hear from seasoned business leaders and academics such as Jack Welch, Jim Collins, Clayton Christensen and others. And books on leadership dominate the list of non-fiction best sellers, many having been translated into dozens of languages. With all this expert advice and teaching available live, in books and on the Internet, what's the problem? Are executives showing up but not listening? Are they buying the books but not reading them?

And leadership-training courses abound, whether they are workshop based, offered over the Internet in digital form, taught in executive MBA schools, or are part of the growing number of offerings by human resource departments inside corporations. And the hallways of modern organizations are clogged with coaches whose job is to improve leadership at all levels of the organization. Yet this growing activity is not producing the required results. Leadership is failing business and the world. What's going on?

The answer lies in the fact that we have been looking at leadership from the wrong end of the telescope and it's been difficult to gain a proper perspective. A vast majority of business books and academic studies in the field of leadership have focused on behavior – behavior styles, communication styles, leadership behaviors, dealing with difficult people, team dynamics, advice from the *'masters'*, and a plethora of other behavior-based approaches. Of course poor or inappropriate behavior in our leaders creates both business and people problems, but is it just the leadership behaviors that need to change?

Teambuilding is a good example. After a 3-day senior teambuilding workshop the improvements in alignment, trust, openness, interpersonal communications and personal change are often spectacular. And the resulting display of renewal, optimism, openness and trust among the senior team usually brings significant improvements in the overall ability to get things done across the company, focus more clearly on business requirements, deal more effectively with people and holds the promise of a more healthy corporate culture.

However, over varying periods of time, often measured in months or one or two quarters at the most, as the glow and healthy attitudes tend to fade, old, non-productive behavior patterns re-emerge and a creeping cynicism sets in. And once a team building or culture change program has failed, it's nearly impossible to try it again – people just aren't up for another short-term spike followed by disappointment. In those rare exceptions where a strong and committed CEO has taken the challenge of behavioral change to heart and leads from the front with demonstrable new behaviors while holding those on the senior team personally accountable, the change in culture has been significantly longer lasting. And consultants and business academics have used these exceptional leaders as justification for the belief that strong leadership behaviors are the solution to business improvement.

After talking with hundreds of senior executives in leadership positions we find that executives are tired of the same old behavioral approaches. Everywhere they turn the books, articles, editorials, blogs, training courses are all pushing the same thing – leadership is failing and leaders need to change their behavior! Is it all a behavior problem? Is there something else we've been missing in our efforts to improve leadership and business performance?

My growing dissatisfaction with the ephemeral nature of behavioral approaches has recently led me on a quest of a different sort – away from business psychology, coaching and leadership training and towards the more tangible, seemingly mundane, less flashy factors associated with organizational performance – I call them leadership work processes. It is my observation that the strongest factors influencing culture, behavior and business performance are the processes that govern work at the top of organizations – a sampling of which includes senior staff meetings, the annual budgeting cycle, the strategic planning process, monthly and quarterly operations reviews, administrative and human resource procedures, capital allocation processes and a host of other business processes driven by the senior team. And in the majority of companies these are not the standardized, replicable, efficient, lean processes that drive consistent business results and demand consistent behaviors to operate and maintain, but a collection of very loose, undefined and in most cases undocumented set of activities.

And if the leadership work processes are not effective, this inefficiency has a magnifying or leverage affect onto the next layers of management and on down into the organization – a phenomenon known as the *'shadow of the leaders'* [33]. While this concept was originally meant to describe how poor leadership behaviors among the senior team (interdepartmental conflict, poor communications, lack of trust, hidden agenda, etc.) are mirrored and magnified down into the organization, I now realize that leadership work-processes, driven by the senior team, can have the same and an even greater negative multiplier effect on the activities and effectiveness of each successive organizational layer.

There is ample evidence that middle managers are frustrated by the inefficiencies of many leadership processes that cause them unnecessary work, excessive time in meetings and additional rework. We now understand that inefficient leadership work processes also inject enormous amounts of waste (time, money, human effort, loss of goodwill) into the organization resulting in slower than adequate strategic and tactical business decisions, lack of ability to follow through or implement new initiatives, cost overruns in important and complex customer delivery programs, low morale and poor employee engagement and commitment.

After observing and studying the transformative impact of lean principles, six sigma methodologies and value chain analysis on performance in manufacturing, supply chain and other business functions, it suddenly became obvious: if we were to look at the senior leadership team as a *'business system'* with a defined set of work processes, this may open up more effective approaches to improve leadership at the top and organization performance in general.

When we began looking at senior leadership teams from this different perspective, something immediately jumped out at us. The leadership team stands apart from the business! They aren't integrated into the business activities they initiate! They are outside the performance improvement game, yet are at the head of the overall corporate value chain!

Normal performance improvement programs have had a great impact on streamlining the efficiency and effectiveness of the work of middle management and certain business functions (lean principles, business reengineering, process redesign, supply chain rationalizations, etc.). But these same improvement concepts have not been applied to the senior team. They are outside the system, not really in the game, aloof from scrutiny and attempts at fundamental improvement and redesign! Either by oversight or intention, they have been left out or opted out. The consequences of leadership disengagement have enormous implications for business effectiveness and organization performance.

If all this sounds vaguely like reengineering revisited, you might be right, but I believe it is more fundamental that just reengineering. The fact is, even though everyone acknowledges that change in the world is only going to accelerate, senior teams have neglected to rethink and change their leadership processes accordingly. And employees, customers and shareholders are paying for it today!

What is the work of the senior team?

The only place where success comes before work is in the dictionary. ~ Donald Kendall, former CEO, Pepsi Co.

In numerous team alignment, strategy and performance improvement workshops over the past two decades we have asked a simple question: *"What is the work of the senior executive team?"*

The answer very much depends on the audience in the room. If the audience is the senior team themselves, the answers come back quickly and with a slight indignation in their voices: develop strategy, control risks, determine budgets, allocate capital to worthy projects, manage talent, maximize profits . . . the list goes on and on. The senior team are accountable for everything! It seems like this group does a huge amount and is no doubt critical to the success of the organization.

And when asked where most of this work takes place, a single answer is predominant – in meetings! Then it tends to dawn on the group: *"If most of our work is conducted in meetings, and we all know meetings are full of wasted time, then how effective is our work?"* As you can imagine, the next several hours in the seminar room are taken up by reflection, lively debate and in many cases, useful insights.

However, if the audience is a group of middle managers or direct reports to the senior team, the answers to that same question, *"What is the work of the senior executive team?"* tend to be very different. First there is characteristically a long pause; you can literally hear the cogs and wheels turning round – a few even snicker under their breath. Then people begin to nervously look around the room, almost urging someone to go first, to throw out the first salvo. It's not infrequent that the silence is broken when someone at the back of the room pipes up: *"Hell if we know!"*

It's not that middle managers don't like or respect the senior team as individuals, although that is the case in some companies, it's more that they are confused by the lack of standardization, documentation and inconsistency of the senior team work processes. As an example, it's not uncommon for direct reports and second level managers to lament that a great deal of their time is taken up chasing data suddenly requested by the senior team: "And once the data goes upstairs it's the last we ever hear of it!"

During our workshop discussions on business improvement and organization effectiveness the topic of reorganizations frequently comes up and the frustration seems to be the same in company after company. In the words of one very concerned second level executive:

> *"When my company experiences performance or delivery problems, instead of looking for root causes and doing a thorough performance and process analysis, the senior team decides to reorganize! New boxes, a couple of new faces, different reporting lines; but the organization still under-performs."*

Here we see a clear example of the erroneous belief that business issues can be solved by getting someone with better leadership (skills and/or behaviors) to own the problem, ignoring the possibility that it might not be a personal leadership defect at all, but rather the result of ineffective business processes at the top.

Leadership Shadows

*Our actions have an eloquence of their own, even when the
tongue is silent. Deeds are far better proof than words.*
~ St. Cyril of Jerusalem

High performance leadership teams understand that their collective and individual behavior casts a positive or negative shadow across the entire organization [33]. And since employees tend to take their cues on what is important and how to behave from watching the behavior of their leaders, negative behavior at the top creates negative behaviors far down into the organization, adversely impacting performance and productivity.

Whether the leadership team is aware of it or not, their behavior casts a powerful shadow far into their organization. And actions speak louder than words! People watch the behavior of their leaders for clues as to what is accepted and what is not. When the leadership team says one thing and then behaves differently employees quickly figure out the real story. One of the major obligations of leadership is integrity between words and deeds!

*Organizations are shadows of their leaders . . .that's the
good news and the bad news!*

When members of the leadership team come into the building and head straight for their offices, head down, not interacting with anyone, that's the story that gets talked about in the canteen and the pubs, not the speech one of them gave on employee engagement and openness. The actions don't match the words. And sometimes no action is really a powerful message. Consider an organization whose culture is characterized by lack of confidence in delivering big projects. *"We always fail to deliver big projects. Remember the SAP implementation three years ago? After spending $20M and tons of management time we cancelled the project. And what about product launches? We never deliver on time and if we do it's full of bugs."*

Why do these limiting and negative beliefs exist inside this company? Simple, because leadership allows them! By not stepping in every time they overhear such comments they are giving tacit support to the negative talk. Leadership is about stepping up, and stepping in! Effective leaders address negative issues head on, inserting different messages, adding positive facts instead of just ignoring the negative talk.

And an even more powerful shadow cast by the senior team is how they interact with each other. If you want teamwork as a core behavior across the organization, it better happen at the top or you won't achieve it anywhere in the company, even with the best teambuilding workshops. If two senior executives don't support each other, you can forget about cross-functional support and cooperation lower down. It was this type of poor leadership shadow that led to the nuclear accident at Three Mile Island in 1979, and countless other examples of suboptimal performance inside organizations.

The files of bankruptcy courts are littered with examples of companies with a good strategy and good people, but poor performance and finally liquidation. It is also true that the same group of executives and employees, who had previously produced dismal results, can, by working well together, turn from loss to profit in short order. Like a car with one or more tires out of balance, poor alignment at the top of an organization can wear down morale, waste energy and eventually tear the company apart. And there cannot be effective strategy implementation without alignment at all levels. But it starts at the top.

I have come to the frightening conclusion that I am the decisive element. It is my personal approach that creates the climate. It is my daily mood that makes the weather. I possess tremendous power to make life miserable or joyous. I can be a tool of torture or an instrument of inspiration. I can humiliate or humor, hurt or heal. In all situations, it is my response that decides whether a crisis is escalated or de-escalated, and a person is humanized or de-humanized. If we treat people as they are, we make them worse. If we treat people as they ought to be, we help them become what they are capable of becoming.
~ Johann Wolfgang von Goethe

Leadership Processes

First we shape out institutions, and then they shape us.
~ Winston Churchill

What do we mean by *'Leadership Processes*? Let's start with the generally accepted definition of a business or work process: **a business process is an organized group of related activities that together create customer value.**

According to Hammer and Champy, *"The focus in a process is not on individual units of work, but rather on an entire group of activities that, when effectively brought together, create a result that delivers customers value."* (Hammer & Champy, *1993).*

Similarly, we are defining a **Leadership Process** as: an organized group of related activities initiated by the senior team and under their direct guidance that together enhances the ability of the senior team to deliver value to their immediate customer.

The key differentiator of a leadership process is that it is initiated and under the guidance of the senior team, and in this case the immediate customer is the management and employees, not the end customer. Leadership Processes are internal activities focusing more on organizational and management effectiveness than on the end customer. Thus, the real customer of the senior team is their direct reports; a notion that has heretofore only been understood and accepted by a few 'enlightened' senior teams.

When defined this way a few of the key leadership processes become immediately obvious; the annual budgeting and periodic review process, the quarterly or monthly operations review process, the annual strategic planning process, senior team staff meetings, the executive talent development process, the employee performance review and appraisal process, and senior staff meetings to name a few. In many ways, these are the work packages of the senior team.

When we ask to see process maps or value stream maps of these processes, few companies can produce them! If they do exist they are not written down to anywhere near the detail and precision as a manufacturing or procurement process. In fact, in most cases leadership processes reside in the collective knowledge of the company and usually the senior executive most closely associated with the issue. For example, the CFO tends to be the owner of the annual budgeting process; the COO owns the operations review process, etc.

In the words of one senior executive:

> *Most of our leadership processes actually work more on tribal knowledge than well designed or documented process steps. And it is hell for a new senior team member – to survive the first year they must rely heavily on their long serving direct reports and other team members who know how things are done. As the old saying goes – the natives have the maps!*

In several cases we have gone into an organization and helped map out one or more of the leadership processes (much like an 'as is' process map at the beginning of a lean transformation on the manufacturing floor), looking for overall flow, time spent at each activity, overall process efficiency and waste. And we have been surprised by what we have found.

First we notice that leadership processes tend to be a patchwork of fixes and changes added on to a legacy process as a way of 'making it work better.' And when the overall time consumed is compared to the actual value-add time, the amount of waste in time, money and human energy is shocking.

One senior executive describes it this way:

> Our budget process is mostly an historical exercise. We take the past 5 years of budget numbers, plug in a growth estimate for each business unit, roll up the figures, then haggle over what we can and can't afford in order to arrive at the three big numbers corporate wants from us in the first place. As a result we spend more time during the year cutting costs and moving allocations around than actually focusing our energies on growing the business in a strategic direction. The waste of time and effort is criminal.

Without standardized, effective and best in class leadership processes, every time a new CEO or leader comes into a company, he /she tends to change things to fit their style or personal way of doing things. Changes in how strategy is developed, how meetings and operations reviews are conducted, how the senior team is structured, and also personnel changes tend to have a negative impact on the momentum of a company. "It's as if everything going on before was wrong and the new way is the right way, except it's never the silver bullet fix intended."

Unfortunately, after two or three successive leadership changes at the top, cynicism tends to invade the ranks of middle management. In one company, after having five CEOs over a 12-year period, a group of disenfranchised middle managers began calling themselves the *'We Be's'*. Digging into this we discovered what it stood for: *"We be here before you, and we be here after you!"* Needless to say their collective resistance to change had a considerable blocking effect on attempts to improve operational performance.

When new leaders bring in new ways of doing things because *"that's the way we did it at my previous company"* or *"it's the way I like to manage"*, without establishing well documented and designed leadership processes, they run the risk of creating greater disenfranchisement among the very employees whose job it is to help improve the company.

Contrast these ad hoc leadership practices with the standardized leadership processes at work in the US Army, often referred to as the *'Mission Command'* [34] process. Here, adherence to standard processes for Planning, Briefing, Executing, and Debriefing can mean the difference between life and death on the battlefield.

If a commander is replaced in the midst of the engagement, there is no time for a 'new way of doing things.' From the General to the platoon Sergeant, everyone knows the standard processes, how they work and how they are to be implemented. In the majority of cases, the process carries the day, not the whims or favorite approaches of the leader. Built into these standard processes however, is the flexibility to respond to unforeseen events with a situational change process that is also well understood at all levels.

Training and Development

> *I hear I forget, I see I remember, I do I understand*
> *~ Confucius*

In former times one of the key leadership processes of the senior team was training and developing the next level of management. Today, like many other processes, this important task has been mostly outsourced, to the human resources function, to executive education courses at prominent business schools, or to an executive coach. In the current economic climate where the rules in play for the past two decades have suddenly been replaced with uncertainty at every turn and many up and coming managers have never had to face such dire business conditions, it is vital that senior management take control of executive development.

However, today's future leaders (General Managers and the like) are not being properly coached by senior leaders. Why? Culprits seem to be the fast pace of business and an ever-increasing senior executive focus on external issues rather than internal. How should this coaching work? This is not about mentoring. This is about real-time coaching and training.

For example, in one company the board and senior leaders saw and sensed the economic slowdown coming, mostly because they have access to experts and outside intelligence that their GMs do not. Knowing it was impossible for them to deal with a mega-downturn through policy alone, they quickly scheduled a 2-day General Manager Strategy Meeting, held at corporate headquarters, where the senior leaders talked to the assembled General Managers about the current and expected future state of their businesses. They shared business examples of best practices and failure modes of businesses, which in similar situations had responded properly, as well as improperly during economic crisis.

Some case studies showed how certain businesses increased investment in key areas, cut COGS, worked margins, and incentivized their best talent. Others cut G&A, stopped investing, and quickly lost their best people. The discussion that followed was pointed, challenging and invigorating. Needless to say that company exhibits an entirely different level of positive energy and feelings of being in control of their destiny than many other companies facing a severe downturn.

Where are the case studies that your general managers and young leaders can read and debate with their senior leaders? And if these case studies exist, where is the willingness of the senior team to enter into such open debates? We see executive development as just one of the many leadership processes that, if properly designed, can yield significant business rewards.

Quality Thinking: The other work of leadership

> *No problem can withstand the assault of sustained thinking.*
> *~Voltaire*

We have only to look at the hassled faces of today's senior executives and scan their daily calendars to realize the majority of time is spent in back-to-back meetings. Meetings often start early in the morning and end late in the evening, with executives running from one to the next, barely taking time for the toilet. It's not that meetings are inappropriate places to conduct executive level business and well-conducted meetings can accomplish a lot. Our concern is that too often meetings are not used for arriving at decisions, collective debate or alignment, but are hijacked by time wasting activities that add little value to the product or the customer.

Michael C. Mankins [16] cites some startling statistics about the use of time among the senior executive team. Analyzing the meeting diaries of senior team members from 187 companies worldwide (with market capitalizations of at least $1 billion), they state the following:

> *The typical company's senior executives spend less than three days each month working together as a*

team – and in that time they devote less than three hours to strategic issues.

What hijacks the majority of the time they spend together in meetings? According to Mankins valuable time is wasted by unstructured processes that address business critical issues in an undisciplined manner. While he introduces examples of seven techniques that can bring some discipline, consistency and effective decision making into senior executive meetings, he stops short of looking at the entire senior team as a system and examining their leadership processes in a robust way.

When processes are ad hoc and undocumented, valuable executive time is taken up either with explanations or debates on issues, which, if the leadership processes were effectively designed, documented and adhered to, would never make it on the agenda. More time would then be available for quality discussion, quality thinking and decision-making.

Harvard Professor Abraham Zaleznik writes: *"Whatever else the real work of leadership involves – and it is constantly changing – it always involves one crucial component. That component is thinking."* [30]

I believe that better designed leadership processes at the top will actually free up senior management time for more quality thinking – alone and together – in their important role as stewards of the company. If we can improve the amount of thinking time senior leaders have, we can also reduce their dependence on outside consultants – after all, who knows more about the company, its strengths, the culture, its customers and the overall business than the senior team? Being able to spend quality time talking together about their business and also have more time for individual thinking can have an enormous impact on the success of the enterprise and is critical to successful strategy execution.

Did you ever stop to think, and forget to start again?
~ Winnie the Pooh

How we got here in the first place

Charisma is the result of effective leadership, not the other
way around. ~ Warren Bennis and Burt Nanus

Why is the senior team outside the corporate value chain? By all reason and logic they should be actively involved in any and all activities that could increase corporate value. Part of the answer lies in the hierarchical model of organization structure advocated by large corporations in the post-war years to manage growth and complexity, and in the common belief that senior leaders are different from the rest of the organization and therefore must stand apart.

But there seem to be at least two other significant contributing factors to lack of leadership engagement. First, Engaged Leadership is very hard work and with all the other time demands on executives, real leadership engagement can easily lose out. Second, is the modern day obsession with the leader as celebrity and the cult of *'executive stardom'*. One of the major by-products of the focus on charisma and exceptional personality as a major determinant of leadership is that people allow and even expect their leaders to be slightly removed from employees and the *'work of the organization'*.

In such a leader-as-celebrity culture, managers respond to ideas from their leaders as infallible pronouncements. In companies where the cult of leadership is strong, few people, even senior executives, speak up or challenge ideas that come from above. As a result for several decades we have been working in an era of *'superstar leadership'* and *'charismatic unaccountability'* where position, title, obscene compensation and attendance at Davos have been substituted for engaged and effective leadership. The poor results are beginning to show.

In his classic research on major corporate disasters and the leaders responsible for them, Sydney Finkelstein [35] cites the *'superstar syndrome'* and *'ineffective leadership practices'* as being at the heart of many spectacular corporate failures. By focusing too much on the CEO, or other superstar executives as the hero *"with all the answers"*, robust leadership processes that can surface valuable information and engage all the members of the leadership team in candid debate tend to take a back seat. Thus the individual superstar who helped orchestrate a spectacular business success several years ago can just as easily lead the company into irrecoverable disaster. This culture of worshiping charismatic leaders tends to over inflate the importance of the individual at the expense of full engagement by the senior team and masks the critical importance of leadership processes on business success.

An Effective Leadership Team . . .

> *Get the right people on the bus, the wrong people off the bus,*
> *and the right people in the right seats.*
> *~ Jim Collins, author of Good to Great*

There are a lot of various beliefs about what constitutes an effective leadership team and, from my point of view, many are just plain wrong!

One of these wrong yet prevalent beliefs has to do with 'hiring the best' and letting them get on with it (note in the Jim Collins quote above he doesn't say the best people, he says the *"right people"*). Hiring a collection of superstars with great track records and polished CVs does not always create a winning team. Just look at professional football in the UK for example. A team full of highly paid superstars may be able to draw large crowds to games and demand higher fees to televise their games, but they don't automatically win a majority of games. There is a difference between being able to play the game expertly and being able to play the game expertly together.

In American baseball, statistics show that the teams with the highest collective player salaries are not usually the league winners, but the winners come from the middle of the pack. So obviously something else is required to finish atop the league tables besides high priced talent.

The same is true of business leadership teams. The highly paid collection of super-talented executives is not always the best leadership team for the business. While recently this has been most evident in banking and financial services, it is actually the case in all industries.

So what else does it take if skill and brains are not sufficient? I keep coming back to the same few essential ingredients for putting together a winning leadership team.

Intrinsic Requirements: Building a successful business leadership team takes more than just skills and technical knowledge.

Effective team members must also bring a set of internal capabilities (values and beliefs):

- Personal values that closely align with a company's core values.
- Communication: They must be able to clearly articulate these values and be willing to promote and spread them to others.

- They are self-directed and don't need to be tightly managed.

- They understand they have a responsibility to achieve results. It's not a job, it's a responsibility they take very seriously. They display a passion for the business to everyone they meet.

- They accept and demand accountability. Their word is their bond and when they commit, you get results, not excuses.

- They have a genuine love of people. They freely give appreciation and respect.

Process Requirements: The second element I find as key to the success of a business leadership team is a management process that encourages individuals to solve business problems together. This is one of the leadership processes I talk so much about as a breakthrough way of working. It's just the opposite of silo-based problem solving. Individuals from various functions who work together tend to solve the problems faster, usually with a simpler solution, and more cost effectively, than relying on individual or subject matter experts.

It is up to the CEO to develop leadership processes that promote team-based approaches to business problems. The Strategy-on-a-Page Execution Roadmap is just such a joined-up leadership and problem solving process.

Take a look at your leadership team. Like what you see? If not, change it.

To truly transform an organization,
you must either change the leaders or change the leaders!

Chapter 23:
Who's On First, What's On Second? . . .
Roles and Responsibilities

However you slice it, lack of management discipline correlates
with poor implementation, and passionate adherence to
management discipline leads to effective implementation.
~ Jim Collins, Good to Great

It is the job of the senior executive leadership team to build, validate, implement, manage and govern the strategy execution process, as well as to lead the teams assigned to develop and deliver strategic initiatives. In essence this requires a different set of behaviors and a reshaped leadership culture. You and the other members of the senior team will now be spending more time on enterprise-wide issues than on the day-to-day running of your function. In order to have the quality time required to truly move the strategy forward and guarantee delivery on milestones and objectives, it is imperative that you delegate much of your day-today functional duties to your next level of management.

Your job now becomes guaranteeing the delivery of the business strategy, not just your functional numbers. Many executives report that their allotment of time shifts from something like 80% Functional – 20% Enterprise to more like 70% Enterprise - 30% Functional issues. As you can imagine, there are some added benefits to this shift. Executives find it stimulating and challenging to be learning more about the entire business (good preparation for future CEOs) and direct reports get the added challenge, responsibility and development that comes with managing the functional issues.

In addition to the shift in focus for the individual members of the senior team, there are specific roles that must be undertaken to better guarantee the delivery of your business strategy.

Role of the Senior Executive Team

The role of the senior executive team shifts more towards leadership of the culture and accountability for the business strategy. In practical terms what this means is that the major focus becomes what's best for the enterprise as a whole. With this shift in mindset comes a new set of behaviors:

- Open sharing of functional information so that all the facts are available
- Listening to all points of view to find the 'best solution', not the best functional solution.
- Supporting and coaching each other
- Being the official spokesperson(s) for the corporate strategy
- Leading employee engagement workshops to communicate the forward strategy
- Helping team members whose projects are falling behind

plan with ideas, people, and resources (every project and strategic initiative needs to be on plan for the entire enterprise to win).

Role of the CEO

The CEO has two very important roles: as a contributing team member to the building of the Strategy-on-a-Page and as the person in charge of running the Strategy Review Meetings. Both roles are critical for the successful delivery of a business strategy.

Too often the mere title of CEO, the *'boss'*, acts to subconsciously suppress open debate and in many cultures it's the boss's ideas that people tend to accept as *'the way it is'*, too often without adequate challenge or debate. While the CEO may have some advantage by being outside the narrow functional point of view, the CEO doesn't have all the right answers. To stimulate open debate and to find the best ideas and solutions the CEO needs to be aware of this dynamic and consciously behave in ways that encourages good debate and open fact-finding among the team.

The CEO chairs the Strategy Review Meetings and he/she is accountable for the success of these meetings by focusing the team on addressing those projects that are missing plan, for resolving project breakdowns, and for monitoring countermeasure activities leading up to the next Strategy Review Meeting.

One of the most important roles of the CEO during the Strategy Review Meetings is to help everyone avoid blame behavior when any of the Strategic Initiatives are missing plan. The most productive behavior is not blame, but teamwork by everyone to help find solutions to get every project back on plan.

In addition, it is critical for the CEO to focus on outcomes and not activities. There are three questions the CEO should continually ask as each person presents the status of their Strategic Initiatives:

- What (specifically) is your next deliverable?
- When (meaning on what date) will you deliver it?
- What support do you need from us in this room to deliver?

By focusing everyone on outcomes and deliverables, the CEO can help build the culture of accountability and performance that is required for effective strategy execution.

Role of the CFO

The Chief Financial Officer (or equivalent) is critical to the success of strategy delivery. Besides being a member of the team during the debates and building of the **Strategy-on-a-Page Execution Roadmap**, more often than not the CFO is selected to oversee the Enterprise Metrics – their validation and reporting. It is critical that these metrics, which are linked directly to the KPIs, be well formulated so that the business is tracking the right measures. The CFO must challenge each one of the draft metrics during its development to ensure validity and applicability to the overall objective. In addition the CFO plays a team role in helping the owners of the Strategic Initiatives to build and validate appropriate metrics and milestones.

Role of the Head of Strategy

In many companies the Head of Strategy is, by default, often assumed to be the owner of the strategy. This is not the case in the *FASTBREAK Strategy Execution* process – the entire team owns the success or failure of the strategy and the individual project owners are accountable for each of the strategic initiatives. The Head of Strategy does play a critical role in the overall formulation of the strategy by helping to dig up as much relevant and factual information as possible on competitors, marketplace trends, niche opportunities, business threats, economic and policy trends, etc. During the debate and building of the Strategy-on-a-Page, it is important to have this information and data available to everyone.

Role of the Strategic Initiative Owner

One of the most critical roles in building the **Strategy-on-a-Page Execution Roadmap** and in delivering on the overall business strategy is the role of the Strategic Initiative owners. This group is comprised of the members of the senior executive team (sometimes with a few key next level leaders) who each become responsible for one or more of the Strategic Initiatives. (Note: our definition of responsibility is not who is to blame when things go wrong, but the person who is most able, willing and committed to respond with whatever it takes to make things right).

When a senior executive is responsible for a Strategic Initiative is means they are the leader of an ad hoc team (usually multifunctional) drawn from various levels in the company that develop a project plan and work that plan until it is completed and the objectives of the initiative are delivered. Choosing the right players to be on the project team is just one important duty and it is often useful to get good subject matter experts as well as people from other disciplines who can bring fresh thinking to the project.

> *Whenever we have a problem we cannot solve, we put together a cross-functional team and I am always amazed at the solutions they come up with.*
> *~ Carlos Ghosn, CEO, Renault and Nissan.*

It is also important that these team members come to this project because they are interested in the issue. It rarely works well if people are chosen for a project without having some degree of interest or commitment, and especially if they see it as a burden; another task on top of the many others. Fresh and creative problem solving ideas normally don't come from resentful people. The very nature of these strategic initiatives is that they often require breakthrough solutions to big challenges.

Another key role of the strategic initiative owner is the reporting of metrics and working with the project team to develop countermeasures (a set of new actions) designed to get the plan back on track when the metrics are falling into the Yellow or Red zone. It is the role of the initiative owner to present his/her results at the Strategy Review Meeting and to be ready to talk about countermeasures as required. It is also important for each Strategic Initiative owner to understand what is happening with each of the other initiatives (which requires paying close attention during the monthly strategy review meetings), since it is often the case that one executive may have a way to help solve another's project problem.

Chapter 24:
CULTURE MATTERS, BIG TIME

*The thing I have learned at IBM is that culture is
everything. ~ Louis V. Gerstner, Jr. former CEO IBM*

A while back I was invited to be a speaker at a meeting of nearly
200 executives of SME Businesses sponsored by the NatWest
Bank. The topic was *Build it, Scale it, Keep it.* What surprised me at
first is why they would chose an expert in corporate culture to sit
in with these obviously highly successful business builders and
entrepreneurs; I was definitely the odd-man in the group. We each
spoke for about 15 minutes and then as a panel, fielded questions.

To my surprise, corporate culture and its importance to
organization success came up time and time again throughout the
evening, both in the questions to the panel and also in the
informal discussions over drinks at the end. The message that
culture matters in all three phases; Building, Growing and Keeping,
is becoming widely accepted.

My presentation focused on the vastly different cultures of

Johnson & Johnson and British Petroleum and how they each responded to deaths associated with their products and the resulting global media attention and legal actions.

Look at the events surrounding the Tylenol poisonings in Chicago in 1982 when 7 people died after a lunatic put cyanide into the capsules of the then leading pain reliever. [36] This tragic event is now a business case study in successfully dealing with crisis. Because of a corporate culture based on the J&J Credo (a nearly 100 year old statement of the company values which puts the customer first and the shareholder last) executives at J&J were open, transparent and fast moving to take all Tylenol products off the market and make certain future products were tamper proof.

Contrast that to the recent 2010 BP Deepwater Horizon oil-rig explosion where 11 people died and 17 were injured. [37] BP is definitely not an open culture and with values firmly focused on cost control and maximizing shareholder value, BP's response and controlled release of information has been vilified in the press and blogs the world over. It is estimated BP faces a decade of lawsuits as people recover from the company's apparent negligence, not to mention having to set aside $20 billion for cleanup and recovery. Along the way the CEO was sacked.

At Johnson & Johnson, then CEO, James Burke, became a business hero for his openness and decisive leadership of the Tylenol crisis. Culture matters, big time ($$ billions).

> *Men do not attract what they want, but what they are.*
> *Organizations do not attract what they plan,*
> *but what they believe about their plans.*

Corporate culture has a tremendous impact on a firm's ability to execute on its strategic objectives. Most strategies deal with ways of beating the competition and growing market share, revenues and profits. The usual approaches are new products, improved quality and speed to market, or rapid expansion to capture first-mover advantage. In all cases, the corporate culture can either act as a propellant, or an anchor.

Are You Driving Blind?

Somebody actually complimented me on my driving today.
They left a little note on the windscreen, it said 'Parking Fine.'
~ Tommy Cooper

There is a funny scene in the movie *If You Could See What I Hear*, based on the life of blind athlete, singer and actor Tom Sullivan, where he is driving a car around his college campus. Remember, Tom is blind from birth. It's a hilarious scene and one of my favorite movies. At one point I lived in Southern California and would bump into Tom (no pun intended) from time to time at a restaurant in Manhattan Beach and we would talk about life and running, among other things. Tom would often say that most people are driving blind, going somewhere fast but not really seeing.

While it may apply to many of us, the questions I often ask CEOs are:

- Are you driving blind?
- Do you really see the culture inside your company?
- Do you see the ways in which corporate culture is hindering your organization?
- Do you see how the behavior and leadership processes of the senior team play a big part in creating your corporate culture?
- Do you see the impact culture has on profitability, customer satisfaction, innovation, productivity, and the wellbeing of your employees?

If you can't answer these questions, it's time to really look. Time to dig in and discover. In many cases you will be very pleased with what you see. In some cases you will be horrified!

George and Harry take a trip

The single biggest problem in communication is the
illusion that it has taken place. ~ George Bernard Shaw

One of the marvels of modern aviation transportation is the autopilot, which on a long distance flight effectively and safely guides the jumbo jet directly to the proper airport and puts it on course for the designated runway landing. This has been of great benefit to long distance travel since the pilots can relax during most of the trip, thus remaining fresh and alert for the important process of landing and maneuvering around weather patterns.

The autopilot process is actually a special relationship between two instruments, the Autopilot, which controls the speed, altitude and direction of the airplane, and the Inertial Navigation System (INS), which is like a GPS, and communicates constantly with the Autopilot about the exact location, speed, altitude and other key bits of information. These two, we can call them George and Harry, are in constant communication as they fly the plane along its preset course. This *'special relationship'* is actually a very sophisticated form of two-way feedback.

Here's how this *'special relationship'* works. Harry (the INS) tells George (the Autopilot) the plane is a little slow and needs to speed up. George says *"thank you"* and makes the corrections. Harry then tells George his needs to increase his altitude. George again says *"thank you"* and makes the altitude adjustment. Harry then tells George they have reached a point where the plane must make a course change. George says *"thank you"* and adjusts the compass bearing. All through the long flight George and Harry are in constant communication and as a result they reach the designated airport safely and effectively.

Now, let's imagine George and Harry were two senior executives, each responsible for a different department or business function. Harry tells George he needs to speed up. George, somewhat incensed that a peer is telling him how to run his area, grudgingly complies. Harry then tells George he is too low and to increase the altitude. George snaps back that Harry should mind his own business. Harry tells George about the upcoming course correction and at this point George stomps off muttering something about how he doesn't have to be told how to run things. Before long Harry and George are not speaking to one another. Or worse, they are both talking to a third executive about each other's rude behavior and now others are negatively impacted.

I wouldn't want to ride on that plane. And I wouldn't want to work in that company either. But because most business executives don't appreciate and understand the value of real-time constructive feedback (they mistake it for criticism), too often meetings are filled with hidden agendas, defensiveness to outside ideas or input, hurt feelings and in a few instances, Vice Presidents not talking to each other.

A good friend of mine, Blackburne Costin, often says: *"Feedback is the Breakfast of Champions."*

No business decision, no project plan, no strategy is ever perfect the first time. As they begin to be implemented they all run into either external change or unexpected obstacles. The most important ingredient in keeping your plans and strategies (and your airplane) on course is constant feedback.

In our leadership alignment and strategy execution workshops we often spend a considerable amount of time practicing the skills of giving and receiving real-time, appreciative and constructive feedback in order to keep things moving forward and to avoid project roadblocks or breakdowns.

If your senior team is not hitting the target, take a look at the amount of feedback passed around and how people respond to direct feedback. In my business experience, teams comfortable with frequent, real-time, information-rich feedback outperform those who focus on their individual functions and keep others (and new ideas) out. And effective strategy execution demands a culture rich in feedback and coaching, at all levels.

SECTION FIVE:
EXECUTION, EXECUTION, EXECUTION

It's character that gets us out of bed, commitment that
moves us into action, but discipline that enables us to win.
~ Zig Ziglar

When asked by a new real estate agent what were the three most important factors in real estate sales, a veteran agent replied: *"Location, Location, Location."* I think a similar reply is true for building a sustainable and growing business: **Execution, Execution, Execution**.

One of the reasons most strategies don't get adequately implemented is because much of the time of the senior team is taken up with day-to-day operational issues and 'firefighting', leaving strategic initiatives to be dealt with by individual project owners who rarely have the authority to make the decisions that can change policies or procedures blocking delivery. As a result, it is easy for strategic initiatives to lose momentum or encounter obstacles that are organizational in nature, such as company policies, etc. When this happens the natural approach is to 'call a meeting' to discuss the issue, decide to inform senior management, which takes time to schedule that meeting, then comes the game of *'whose problem is it?'* and the natural turf protection that follows. All the while the project grinds to a slow crawl and the team gets discouraged with the lack of momentum and slow decision making.

To keep the strategy on track and to ensure timely delivery of strategic initiatives, the **FASTBREAK Strategy Execution** process includes a standing Strategy Review Meeting (SRM) with the senior executive team and all the Strategic Initiative owners. Unless the senior team is fully engaged and ultimately accountable, Strategic Initiatives run the risk of becoming just another set of conflicting priorities among all the other demands for resources. Holding the Strategy Review Meetings frequently helps maintain focus and momentum and attacks blockages to the strategy early before they become insurmountable obstacles and before valuable time is lost.

Once the **Strategy-on-a-Page Execution Roadmap** has been completed and loaded with the appropriate information, it then becomes the focal point for the Strategy Review Meetings. The purpose of the Strategy Review Meeting is to:

- Acknowledge and appreciate those strategic initiatives that are on track (GREEN)
- Focus on those strategic initiatives that are not progressing (either RED or YELLOW)
- Make certain the overall Key Business Metrics are moving in the right direction.
- Initiate countermeasures as appropriate

NOTE: The Strategy Review Meeting is not an update, a report-out meeting, or a *'tick-the-box'* activity. Don't attend expecting to check your messages and do email until it's your turn to present!

The Strategy Review Meeting is designed to focus the talent, knowledge, and decision-making authority of the organization on moving the strategy forward, and as such, it is a highly participative and interactive set of discussions that result in specific countermeasures and actions by the appropriate individuals accountable.

It is important for the entire senior team to be engaged in these discussions to help solve problems that arise across the organization and to avoid 'silo' focused actions that tend to create suboptimal solutions and interdepartmental conflicts.

Establishing a new 'management discipline'

Discipline is the bridge between goals and accomplishments.

The Strategy Review Meeting requires the establishment of a new discipline among the management team and throughout the entire company. To be effective, the SRM must become a standard work practice (leadership process) and not just a series of meetings that take place when it is convenient. If you want the strategy to be delivered, then it will be the result of aligned leadership and disciplined management.

Making the SRM a 'way of life' will not be easy, particularly because day-to-day operating crises tend to compete for management's attention. Additionally, to be effective, the SRM requires pre-work on the part of all participants. The strategy can't be adequately progressed if people just show up to the meeting and '*wing it*'. For those strategic initiatives in the Yellow or Red, the pre-work requires a detailed root cause analysis prior to the meeting and a Recovery Plan to be drawn up so that it can be discussed with the entire group. This is another good discipline that will help in effective strategy implementation.

It is up to the CEO to lead by example and make the SRM important to the success of the business. For example, when is it appropriate to cancel or postpone a SRM? The answer is never! If there is a *'save the company'* emergency happening that very day, then by all means, move the time of the meeting till after the crisis. Otherwise, the CEO must impress upon people that they structure their work around the SRM, not restructure the SRM to fit around other work.

> *A culture of discipline is not a principle of business;*
> *it is a principle of greatness. ~ Jim Collins*

Chapter 25:
CADENCE: REGULAR STRATEGY REVIEW MEETINGS

*Nothing can be more hurtful to the service, than the neglect
of discipline; for that discipline, more than numbers, gives
one army the superiority over another.*
~ George Washington

My daughter is a blossoming young solo violinist and has been taking lessons since the age of 6 years old. At her level of play she is now attacking complicated violin concertos and sonatas by the heavyweight classical composers and some of the passages are devilishly complex to master. A few weeks ago she went to a lesson with her violin professor complaining that she just couldn't get this one particular passage. He looked at the score, then looked at her and asked: *"And how many times have you tried it?"* *"Three"* she replied.

In our modern world of speed and instant gratification, we expect results immediately, if not sooner. When most executive teams start down the road to effective strategy execution, they unwittingly expect results to *automagically* materialize. After all, we've done the planning.

The same is true for Strategy Review Meetings. Executives expect to be in and out in about an hour, all the initiatives moving along as planned, and little interaction, just delivering your report card when called on. But effective strategy execution is a discipline and one that must be practiced regularly.

What is the best cadence for Strategy Review Meetings? We recommend every two weeks, with a duration of 3-4 hours. Now, before you fall off your chair and complain that you don't have time for another meeting, just sit back and calculate the cost of not delivering your strategic objectives. Believe me, once you have gotten into the discipline of frequent Strategy Review Meetings, you will understand the value. And you think every two weeks is overkill? Alan Mulally held weekly 3-hour review meetings for over two years during the turnaround of Ford Motor Company. And every senior executive had to attend, in person or electronically, globally!

The strength of the Strategy Review Meeting as an execution tool lies in the regular updates of the Strategic Initiative milestones and the KPI metrics. It is through the color-coding (R-Y-G) system that the senior team is able to focus on issues and solve problems standing in the way of effective strategy delivery. The R-Y-G (RED, YELLOW, GREEN) coding system is a visual identifier for:

- GREEN = On target (0 to 7% off plan)
- YELLOW = Concern (8% to 15% off plan)
- RED = Critical Issue (> 15% off plan)

(Note: you should select your own intervals for breakpoints between Green – Yellow – Red indicators. These are only suggested intervals but seem to work well for most organizations)

Preparing for the Strategy Review Meeting

I am always ready to learn
although I do not always like being taught.
~ Winston Churchill

One week before the meeting the CEO or designated Chairperson should send out a reminder about the upcoming meeting with location and times. Remember, this is a standing meeting that is scheduled for a rolling 12 months, so everyone should already have the date, time and location in their calendars.

Here are some useful pre-meeting guidelines:

- **Designated Stand-In:** Anyone not able to make the meeting either physically or electronically should notify the chairperson immediately with the name of the designated stand-in and the issues that person will be dealing with. It is critical that the stand-in be well prepared since this is a problem solving meeting not a reporting session!

- **Updates:** All updates to Strategic Initiatives and Key Business Metrics must be input into the Plan-on-a-Page Execution Roadmap several days before the SRM.

- **Pre-meeting Review:** the Chairperson should review the updated execution roadmap and be prepared to manage the discussion

Establishing Clear Objectives and Ground Rules for the SRM

If you don't know where you are going, any road will get
you there. ~ Lewis Carroll

The Strategy Review Meeting occurs regularly (twice-monthly is suggested) and is critical to effective strategy execution. The best and most productive meetings are those with clear objectives and ground rules. It is imperative that all those attending the SRM understand the objectives of the meeting.

Suggested SRM objectives:

- Review and improve strategy delivery plans
- Bring the talent and wisdom of the team to bear on underperforming Strategic Initiatives
- Provide enough ideas and suggestions for the Initiative owner to improve their project plans to help get his/her initiative back into the GREEN.
- Acknowledge progress and ensure organizational learning
- Gather up lessons learned – group learning

A meeting is only as good as its ground rules and the behavior of the participants. Clearly understood ground rules and an agreed set of appropriate behaviors can help ensure effective meeting dynamics and a productive outcome.

Suggested Strategy Review Meeting Ground Rules and Behaviors:

- Meeting starts and ends on time. Duration is 3-4 hours (specified) unless otherwise changed ahead of time.
- Everyone must attend either physically or via conference call (video link is preferred).
- Any substitutes or stand-ins must be well briefed and prepared beforehand and have good knowledge of the issues. "*I don't know about this*" or "*I am not familiar with the issue/data*" is not acceptable. Come prepared since this is not a report out session but a time to help move the strategy forward.
- All smartphones, cell phones and other communication devices turned off and remain off throughout the meeting.
- One scheduled 15 minute break half way through
- This is a team activity and everyone should be engaged in

all discussions to get all the talent focused on solving important strategy issues

- Look for the best overall solution for the company – put company needs above individual or department objectives

- Meeting facilitator keeps time and ensures the flow of the meeting towards a productive outcome

- Do not try and solve a particular problem during the meeting – gather ideas and input so the initiative owner can build a recovery plan after the meeting

- Make clear commitments with end dates and accountabilities

- Bring a win-win team attitude to the meeting

- It's okay to disagree but not to be disagreeable

- Live by the company values and your written leadership team behaviors

Conducting the Strategy Review Meeting

I think there needs to be a meeting to set an agenda for more meetings about meetings. ~ Jonah Goldberg

The following is a suggested outline for conducting a Strategy Review Meeting, but feel free to adjust to suit your company and situation.

- Welcome

- Review Meeting Time deadlines, objectives and ground rules

- CEO's remarks on significant business events or corporate activities past and coming up

- Appreciation: recognize one or two employees for outstanding performance (actually bring the employee into the meeting room to receive his/her recognition. Having the entire senior team recognize above and beyond achievements by an employee is a good process for building a culture of recognition).

- Display and give overview of up-to-date strategy results: show the current **Strategy-on-a-Page Execution Roadmap** and Enterprise Metrics.

- Ask the KPI owner(s) to quickly review the status of the KPIs

- Acknowledge GREEN Strategic Initiatives: Ask for any key insights as to why these are green, lessons learned, etc.

- Review of each RED and YELLOW Strategic Initiative by Initiative Owners (manage the time to get to review all RED and YELLOW initiatives in the time allotted)

  o Initiative owner summarizes current situation

- Root cause assessment of the problem

- Planned recovery actions

  o Group Discussion: Suggestions, Ideas and Offers of Support

  o Initiative Owner: Summary of next steps

- Next Steps: Explain that all RED and YELLOW initiatives must have a revised approach, with countermeasures by the end of the week to be reviewed with CEO or COO.

- End meeting with appreciation

Chapter 26:
DEALING WITH 'BREAKDOWNS'

Although you may face setbacks, change, crisis, and tough times,
you are still accountable for meeting your goals.
~ Jim Lovell, Apollo 13 astronaut

A strategic initiative in the RED or YELLOW zone is not on track and is missing its planed metrics or objectives. We call this a Breakdown, because in one way or another the team accountable for the success of this initiative is not delivering on its performance commitment and something is getting in the way. No one sets out to underperform so we must assume there is either a physical or mental barrier, or a combination of the two.

There are two ways of dealing with Breakdowns. Too often, managers or team leaders take the easy way out and decide that because the team is 'working hard' and the best course of action is to shift the objective or revise the goal. The fact is, all change is hard and all new initiatives face technical and business difficulties, as well as human resistance to change. It's supposed to be hard, otherwise we would have done it already and it wouldn't really be a Breakthrough, but just an incremental improvement.

The only effective way to deal with a schedule or goal breakdown is through Renewed Commitment and Innovation. With this approach and mindset, Breakdowns are seen as opportunities to re-examine the process that generated them and learn to work together more effectively. Renewed Commitment means a stubborn unwillingness to give up or give in, and Innovation means finding a different way to solve the problem and work together. Get creative, get committed, and find new ideas and approaches.

A Breakdown is the necessary and natural precursor to a Breakthrough. The inevitable shift from Breakdown to Breakthrough is almost always heralded by a shift of focus from complexity to simplicity; a return to the fundamentals or the basic principles of what we are trying to accomplish. Often solutions can be fostered by talking with people 'outside' of the problem, from other departments or other functions who might be able to help us see things differently.

First, achieving a Breakthrough takes belief; belief that there is 'something' about the problem we are confronted with that will add value for our company or our customers. Second, breakthrough is more about hard work than thinking up a new idea. It's more about execution than inspiration. Start trying things and you will almost always find a new insight into the solution. And third, it is important to get rapid feedback during the process. Fail fast and fail often when trying to develop a breakthrough – don't analyze it to death!

It's the role of the Strategic Initiative Owner to help guide and push the team through the Breakdown to create a Breakthrough. It is the role of the CEO not to renegotiate goals or objectives but to support and encourage the search for true Breakthroughs.

Chapter 27:
FROG IN A RUT AND EFFECTIVE STRATEGY EXECUTION

If you think you can do a thing or think you can't do a thing, you're right. ~ Henry Ford

This is one of my favorite stories that I use during our Strategy and Execution Workshops. It always elicits hearty laughter, then a quiet silence as the real message sinks in.

> *Once upon a time there was a little frog hopping through the forest when he came upon a muddy logging road. It rained heavily in the forest and the road had deep ruts created by the frequent logging trucks that travelled from the forest to the paper mills.*
>
> *As the little frog jumped across the road he realized, too late, that the ruts were wider than his leap and he landed at the bottom of one of the ruts. The frog was small and the rut deep and hard as he tried he couldn't jump out.*
>
> *He them hopped a long distance in both directions, only to*

discover that the rut was endless (much like most ruts we find ourselves in). He sighed, sat down and gave up. "Stuck in a rut," he muttered to himself.

Just then a big Bull Frog came hopping along and noticed the little frog at the bottom of the rut. "What you doing down there, little frog?"

"Stuck in a rut. I can't get out."

"Well, sorry but I can't help you. I'm on my way to the pond to catch some flies and squeeze me some girl frogs." And the Bull Frog hopped away.

A little while later, while the big Bull Frog was sunning himself on a rock at the edge of the pond the little frog hopped up next to him. "I thought you were stuck in a rut," said the Bull Frog.

"I was," quipped the little frog.

"I thought you couldn't get out."

"I couldn't," replied the little frog, grinning and catching a fly with his tongue.

"So? What happened?" asked the Bull Frog.

"Well, I had to get out, a truck was coming!"

It's amazing what we can do when we decide it's really important! Every time I work with a senior team during a turnaround or the development of a new strategy I am reminded of the little frog. Results are really about choice. Do we want the result bad enough or do we find enjoyment and comfort in complaining? My tutor used to say there are only REASONS or RESULTS. And it all begins with a choice.

The power of frequent Strategy Review Meetings lies in three important principles of effective strategy execution.

The First is Transparency.

The Truth is the only thing you'll ever run into that has no agenda. ~ Adyashanti

Nothing is hidden during the Strategy Review Meeting, everything is '*up on the table.*' There is no '*invisible elephant*' in the room. The **Strategy-on-a-Page Execution Roadmap** lays out the strategy and the current performance on a single page, everything is there for all to see, completely transparent. All the initiatives are color-coded, as well as the names of the initiative owners. A quick scan and everyone knows which initiative (and which owner) needs help. The KPIs have been updated and color-coded and a click on the appropriate information cell explodes all the relevant data pertaining to that KPI. Issues are easily and quickly surfaced and dealt with in the open.

And that's the good news. Because the more people know about an issue or a problem, the greater the probability that someone will have a solution based on past experience, or have seen a similar situation either here or at another company. Given the right leadership culture and teamwork, ideas come out quickly and the initiative owner then just needs to follow up with the various individuals after the meeting and begin to formulate countermeasures.

However, when a senior team embarks upon regular strategy review meetings, it's not always so easy to get all the real information. There is a little human thing called pride and not wanting to be the one who can't deliver.

Alan Mulally, CEO of Ford Motor Corporation, tells a story of the first turnaround review meetings he conducted as the senior team was trying to get traction on their turnaround plans. For the first several weeks, everything was coded as '*on plan.*' Finally, after several weeks of *'on target'* charts and little honest and transparent discussion, Mulally asked a question: "*If everything is on track, then why are we losing billions and why do our customers hate us?*"

According to Mulally, next week, Mark Fields, Head of Ford Operations of North America, admitted that one of his biggest strategic initiatives was *'off plan.'* Alan stood up and clapped. That broke the ice and people realized that telling the truth wasn't going to end in a public lynching, as in previous Ford cultures. Then another executive spoke up and related that his region had faced a similar problem and went on to describe their successful approach.

Transparency of the problem, combined with a growing culture of teamwork at the top, led to a breakthrough for Ford North America. According to Mulally that was a breakthrough moment for the Ford leadership team and I suspect, a breakthrough in the turnaround process at Ford.

The Second is Frequency

If you're coasting, you're either losing momentum or else you're headed downhill.

Holding the Strategy Review Meetings with a regular frequency, say every two weeks, establishes the momentum required to deliver on longer-term initiatives. With a regular frequency, issues can be addressed sooner and solutions found faster.

Within most companies, the frequency for strategy review meetings is generally once a quarter (every three months). First of all, it takes a week to prepare for these meetings, as new slides have to be made, information gathered, and teams assembled to 'practice their pitch' for the review. Beside the time lost to preparation, issues that may block the forward progress of a particular strategic initiative tend to get lost during the previous three months due to daily firefighting and customer problems.

While everyone comes out of the Quarterly Strategy Review with good intentions, knowing that the next review is three months away drains the sense of urgency that is required to keep moving the strategy forward. Imagine if there was only one huddle every quarter in a football game. The rest of the time would be knee-jerk reactions rather than the methodical power of the long drive to the end zone.

The Third is Flexibility

In preparing for battle I have always found
that plans are useless, but planning is indispensable.
~ General Dwight D. Eisenhower

One of the key features of the **Strategy-on-a-Page** process is its flexibility. In today's uncertain and rapidly changing global business environment it is not unusual for something to happen within your marketplace that will have a significant impact on a portion of your business strategy. Perhaps one of your competitors introduces a new product that no one expected or worse yet starts a price war. Perhaps there is a major political upheaval in one of your key foreign markets. Perhaps there is additional unforeseen fallout from the recent global financial meltdown. Unfortunately, the list is long and often very scary.

It would be nice if your strategic planning was built on 100% accurate foresight and had previously developed alternative scenarios for all the potential mega-changes, but that's not realistic. What is realistic however is to quickly pinpoint those few Strategic Initiatives on your current **Strategy-on-a-Page Execution Roadmap** that are negatively impacted and adjust them accordingly, rather than having to scrap the entire strategic plan and start over. Because everyone in the company clearly understands the key breakthrough objectives and their linked strategic initiatives and projects, it is relatively easy to get a group together to make the proper adjustments to those initiatives most impacted by marketplace shifts.

SECTION SIX:
BUILDING CRITICAL MASS

The real power of strategy lies in its ability to seduce.
~ Jeanne Liedtka

There is a fabulous article in Chapter 8 of Henry Mintzberg's book, *Strategy Bites Back,* by Jeanne Liedtka, currently on the faculty of the Darden School of Business at University of Virginia and former chief learning officer at United Technologies Corporation. The title says it all: *"Strategy as the art of seduction."*

Professor Liedtka argues that for a company strategy to be internally effective and get the entire employee body engaged, it has to appeal to everyone in the organization. It has to be so "seductive" in its vision and ideas as to compel employees to want to support and help implement the strategy. She argues that it's not so much about having a perfect strategy, but instead whether the strategy story is *"compelling enough to seduce you and make* you want to be part of it."

I can hear the questions: *"Just what do you mean by the strategy story? I thought the power of a strategy lay in its analytical rigor, clear thinking, and market understanding? You mean it has to have story as well?"*

Humans are story-telling creatures. Take this early-man scenario.

> One of the members of the tribe has an idea on how to get meat. Simple. Sharpen some sticks, go out into a heard of huge Wooly Mammoths and jab one with the sticks until it is dead.
>
> With that type of a sales pitch the obvious reaction is: "Are you nuts?"
>
> So, our cleaver huntsman creates a story to entice his fellow hunters into joining the venture.
>
> He talks not about the dangers, the long marches, the freezing cold, the crushing feet and huge tusks, but about how big and strong their children will grow with plenty of meat. How they will be revered around the campfire for their courage. How the tribe will prosper. How their exploits will be drawn on the cave walls for all to see and remember their courage.

Stories were developed for two purposes: to pass on tribal knowledge and to get people to do difficult things that needed to be done.

It could be argued that the strategy story is the most important story in your entire organization, and so it must also be the most compelling. The strategy story should bring the strategy to life for people and help make it personal to them.

What is compelling about your strategy? Think about the benefits gained, not the problems to be solved. Build a mental picture and a story of how customers will benefit, how growth and success will positively impact everyone, how success will bring the opportunity for more advancement and more interesting work. Talk about the satisfaction gained by delivering solutions faster and better than anyone else. The story is there, you just have to bring it out!

For a good overview of executive-level stories, see Paul Smith's recent book: *Lead with a Story.*

Obstacles are those frightful things you see
when you take your eyes off the goal. ~ Henry Ford

Chapter 28:

COMMUNICATION, EMPLOYEE ENGAGEMENT AND INNOVATION

The world is changing very fast. Big will not beat small anymore. It will be the fast beating the slow. ~ Rupert Murdoch

In today's fast-cycle business environment, there's no time for the 'trickle-down' process of communication. Results must be obtained quickly. And quick results are only achieved when the entire organization is mobilized and focused on specific deliverables that relate directly to the business strategy. If the energy, enthusiasm, ideas and spirit of all employees can be released, it is amazing how quickly things change and results begin to happen, often with extraordinary outcome!

A 12-month Towers Perrin study of 50 financial organizations found a strong relationship between engagement and business results. The organizations with high levels of engagement outperformed the companies with low levels of engagement in three important measures of financial performance: operating income, net income and EPS. High-engagement companies saw a 19.2% increase in their operating income over the 12-month study, while low-engagement companies saw a 32.7% decline. [4]

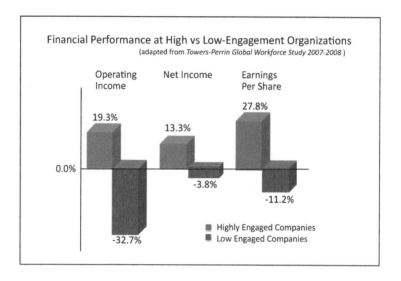

Financial Performance at High vs Low-Engagement Organizations
(adapted from *Towers-Perrin Global Workforce Study 2007-2008*)

An effective way of capturing the hearts and minds of employees is to get them actively involved in the strategy execution process. Give them a voice, give them accountability, give them recognition and feedback and they will propel your company forward. Revising the traditional strategy communication process from the one-way broadcast approach to a series of engaging dialogues is a major component of effective strategy execution. And it must be leader-led! The senior team must facilitate and communicate in these workshops. It's not the role of HR, the Communications Department, or outside facilitators. It's the most important role the senior team has – engaging and enrolling the entire organization in implementing the business strategy.

So, why is employee communication normally left to HR or the Communications Department? First, it's hard work. It takes time, it takes preparation and it takes listening - perhaps the hardest skill of all. And secondly, most senior executives are somewhat intimidated by the role of *facilitating genuine two-way dialogue.'* It's easy to stand up and give a PowerPoint show-and-tell presentation then ask for questions at the end (usually there are few because most of the audience is brain dead by that time).

It's much more difficult to show up authentically, as a facilitator, and share your own insights and concerns about the plan and to engage employees in an honest dialogue about the future of the company. But be prepared, it may be hard work and takes some training, yet at the end of these workshops most senior managers leave the room feeling 10 ft tall and at the same time humbled by the wisdom and energy in the room.

Too often the communication program for strategy deployment involves video messages from headquarters, e-mails, or a mention at the weekly management meeting. These often raise more questions than answers. And the biggest question of all: *"What does this mean to me?"* rarely gets answered sufficiently to motivate people towards implementation. But with a little creativity it is relatively easy to make the communication process engaging and inspiring.

For example, at one large telecoms company, the IT group needed to shift the way they designed software, from the classic waterfall method to an agile software methodology, in order to support the company's strategy of being quicker to market and more customer driven. After nearly a year of putting in place skill training, CBT courses and a massive reorganization, morale and productivity had plummeted. The question being asked was: *"How do we get people engaged to deliver on the new strategy?"*

A quick assessment of the culture within the IT groups found much confusion and rumor about what was expected of them and how they were supposed to work. Rather than just responding with *"we've told them a thousand times",* we suggested the senior team provide leadership and become facilitators of the change process. They took the corporate strategy and built a series of compelling stories, each told by one of the senior executives, which put the entire change strategy into the words and world of IT. Using the Strategy-on-a-Page as the central focus, they organized and facilitated 1-day workshops for all 8,000 employees (100 employees at a time) and facilitated the workshops using an open, honest process of real two-way dialogue. They even brought in customers to talk about their needs. Power points were banned in favor of dialogue! Interactive discussions replaced 'executive presentations.'

The results? Besides a growing employee enthusiasm and renewed respect for management and the company, changes quickly began to come together and the next year IT delivered on all its major strategic commitments, and with a reduced headcount as well.

Engagement and Innovation

> To win in the marketplace you must first win in the
> workplace. ~ Doug Conant, CEO of Campbell's Soup

If you believe that senior management has the best insight into the business and the customer, think again. They may eventually understand the changing dynamics of the market and the evolving needs of the customer (after enough data comes in), but employees are closest to the customer and see changes first.

A successful strategy should evolve to meet the changing needs of customers and the market as quickly as possible to gain and keep competitive advantage. But the sad fact is, many senior managers become aware of fundamental customer changes far too late in the game and run the risk of falling behind more nimble competitors or new entrants who are tapping into those changes.

If you believe that the smartest people in the company must be at the top of the organization and therefore most good ideas come from these few, you tend to get a distribution of ideas or solutions that looks like the standard power or logarithmic curve.

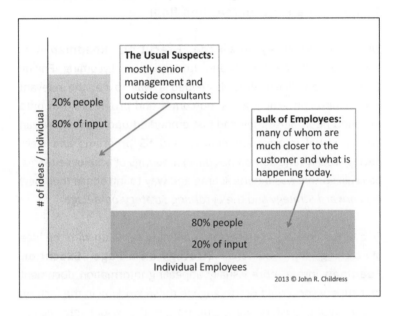

In most companies the 'usual suspects', mostly senior management and consultants, tend to produce most of the ideas and input on the business strategy and how to beat the competition. Only a few ideas come from the bulk of the employee body.

This curve may accurately depict the number of ideas, but it says nothing about the **QUALITY** of the ideas! It is our experience that employees, especially those closer to the customer or closer to the problem, may actually have better solutions. But most organizations don't have an efficient or effective way to engage employees in the strategy nor gather the potential great ideas and solutions that may exist among employees. Using the **Strategy-**

on-a-Page as the one common document for strategy and business discussions makes it easy to get employees at all levels engaged in bringing forth ideas and solutions to improve the business.

Strategy-on-a-Page on the shop floor

When the **Strategy-on-a-Page Execution Roadmap** was complete and the turnaround underway at Lycoming Engine Company, Ian Walsh, VP/GM, needed a way to get the relevant information concerning goals, outcomes and progress down onto the shop floor. Since they had just embarked upon several Kaizan events, visual information boards, and 5S programs and were having weekly (and sometimes daily) meetings of employee teams, he realized this was a natural time and way to introduce their new *Go Forward Strategy* and the *Lycoming Strategy-on-a-Page*.

One of the creative managers in marketing came up with the idea of turning the traditional **Strategy-on-a-Page Execution Roadmap** into a more visually appealing information document that supervisors could use to engage those working in the factory. The resulting posters were put up on the visual information boards spread around the factory floor and supervisors would hold short Q&A sessions about one or more of the strategic objectives. In short order employees began to understand how the work they were doing in assembly, test, receiving and inspection, or maintenance was contributing to the overall turnaround of the company.

Below is a copy of the Lycoming Employee Strategy map.

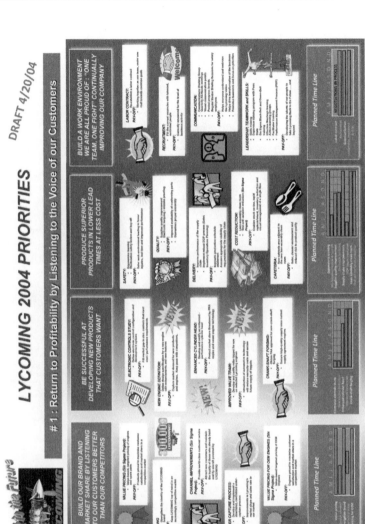

SECTION SEVEN:
Q&A ABOUT FASTBREAK STRATEGY EXECUTION

Over the past several decades of helping senior teams improve their strategy execution capabilities, there have naturally been some common concerns and questions. In this section I have highlighted some of the most frequent concerns and our attempts to respond appropriately.

Question 1
What is the difference between the *FASTBREAK Strategy Execution* process and Kaplan and Norton's *Balanced Scorecard* approach?

Answer:
There are many similarities, especially in the fundamental

principles behind effective strategy execution. The principle of line-of-sight, the principle of visual mapping and the principle of a balanced set of business categories are prominent in both approaches.

However, we have built the *FASTBREAK Strategy Execution* process to include several critical elements missing in most other approaches, including the Balanced Scorecard. These important elements are leadership team alignment, culture change and an understanding of human behavior and organization dynamics. In addition, there is a large dose of Lean methodology (philosophy and tools) imbedded in the *FASTBREAK Strategy Execution* process.

Question 2

The process seems very mechanical and almost rigid. Won't this approach stifle creativity and innovation?

Answer:

Creativity and innovation is the lifeblood of most companies. Our experience is that the *FASTBREAK Strategy Execution* process actually enhances innovation since it allows all levels of the company to better understand the goals and objectives and to engage in meaningful improvement discussions. This process also encourages a large dose of customer engagement, a source of many new innovative ideas.

One value that comes from this structured approach to strategy execution is the management discipline that is developed over time. It is only through discipline and follow-through that innovative ideas can gain traction. Too many companies are long on ideas and short on follow-through.

Question 3

How do I get my senior team to focus on the strategy more than their functional objectives?

Answer:

It is extremely difficult to develop the enterprise focus and cross-functional teamwork required for successful strategy execution when senior executives are so focused on delivering functional goals.

The wise old saying: *"If you want to get someone's attention, fiddle with their wallet."* holds true for senior teams. Alan Mulally at Ford eliminated all functional bonuses for his senior team. Their entire variable compensation depended on how well the company delivered on its overall strategic objectives.

A less radical approach is to shift the focus, with a much larger percentage of variable compensation on strategy execution and a lesser percentage from functional results.

In either case, it is important to staff your senior team with those who have the intrinsic values of *'company first.'* Otherwise excessive personal agenda and selfish behavior can slow down the strategy execution process.

Question 4

Having a Strategy Review Meeting every two weeks seems like a lot of extra meetings. We are already *'maxed'* out with meetings.

Answer:

Meeting effectiveness is often the real issue behind the notion of *'too many meetings.'* The Strategy Review Meeting guidelines provide for an effective, fast moving, and action oriented set of discussions. Experience has shown that twice monthly Strategy Review Meetings often clear up issues that other less effective meeting formats don't and in many cases the result is a reduced number of meetings, since those with authority are in the room and decisions can be made, rather than the normal approach of 'schedule another meeting'.

Question 5

I would like to use the **Strategy-on-a-Page** as an employee communication tool but it looks very complicated and might turn off employees.

Answer:

At first, the **Strategy-on-a-Page Execution Roadmap** is a little overwhelming, but certainly not as overwhelming as a 60-slide PowerPoint presentation. There is a *'line-of-sight'* logic in the layout of the **Strategy-on-a-Page** and once that is understood, the overall picture makes sense to people. Also, the best way to get employees to understand your strategy is to engage them in a dialogue about the various elements of the strategy (People, Products, Operations, Marketplace, Finance) and how they all work together.

Also, taking a clue from Lycoming and producing a more engaging employee version of the **Strategy-on-a-Page** works very well. The key to employee engagement with the strategy is frequent updating of the information and regular discussions and briefings on progress and challenges in execution.

Question 6

How do we get the appropriate data linked to the **Strategy-on-a-Page?** Is this complicated and does it require lots of time?

Answer:

Most companies build their **Strategy-on-a-Page Execution Roadmap** using PowerPoint and then hyperlink the various cells to Excel data that already exists or they use the common templates shown in this book. In either case, hyperlinking documents and data to the cells on the **Strategy-on-a-Page** makes the information readily accessible and not difficult to update on a monthly or twice a month basis.

Question 7

My company is not in a turnaround situation. It seems that the **FASTBREAK Strategy Execution** process is skewed towards turnarounds.

Answer:

Speed, focus and discipline are vital in a turnaround, but no less so than in a healthy company competing in today's complicated and fast moving global marketplace. A turnaround has the added luxury (accompanied with added pain) of focusing everyone's attention on survival and speedy decision-making. The **FASTBREAK** process brings these attributes of focus, discipline and speed to healthy and growing companies, which makes them even more agile and competitive.

Question 8

What is the best time in the business cycle to implement a new strategy and strategy deployment process?

Answer:

That depends on a lot of factors, but if you feel that your current strategic objectives and strategic initiatives are not getting traction or that there is not enough discipline or focus on strategy execution, then the best time is now. Competitors are not going to wait, they are moving now to take your customers and market position. In less turbulent times there was logic in refreshing a strategy at year-end. The sooner you refocus your senior team and align the organization around a robust strategy execution process the better.

Question 9

I am a CEO and it is obvious that I need to change out a few members of my senior team. Should I start this process now or wait till I get the new team assembled?

Answer:

It would be ideal if we had the perfect team on board with which to collectively develop and implement our strategy, but that seldom is the case. Even if you have a perfect team, chances are someone will get poached or choose to move on, and you will have new players joining the team. Get started now and two things will happen. First, one or more of your underperformers might just rise to the occasion now that there is a disciplined and robust strategy execution process in place. Secondly, those who cannot or choose not to perform become very obvious to everyone and the discussion to part company becomes straightforward.

Question 10

Can my team and I implement the *FASTBREAK Strategy Execution* process and **Strategy-on-a-Page Execution Roadmap** on our own, or do we need outside consulting help?

Answer:

The mechanics of setting up and implementing the **Strategy-on-a-Page** are fairly straightforward and any Excel or PowerPoint 'jockey' on your team can put the templates and formats together and use hyperlinks to attach the appropriate material.

Where you might find outside support useful is to have a consultant with considerable experience in strategy discussions and how to establish meaningful breakthrough objectives and KPIs that work. In addition, a team facilitator with experience in strategy and senior team dynamics can greatly improve the quality of your senior team's work together.

SECTION EIGHT:
RUN LIKE HELL!

Your success in life isn't based on your ability to simply change. It is based on your ability to change faster than your competition, customers and business.
~ Mark Sanborn

This is an old joke, but it has a very powerful message for the CEO in executing a competitive strategy:

> *Two backpackers were on a remote trail in the Alaskan wilderness when they rounded a corner and came upon a very agitated Grizzly Bear. One of the hikers turned and fled, yelling "Run for your life!"*
>
> *The other calmly sat down, quickly removed his heavy hiking boots and put on his running shoes. Looking back the fleeing hiker screamed, "What are you doing, you can't outrun a Grizzly?"*

The other hiker replied: "I don't have to outrun the bear, I just have to outrun you."

When is your strategy finished?

The real answer is . . . never! There is no perfect strategy that once formulated, can be put into motion and left alone. Bears (aka competitors) are constantly popping up around the corner, ready to have you for lunch. Reacting with speed and market intelligence is critical.

Chapter 29:
"Once More Unto The Breach, Dear Friends!"
- The Annual Planning Cycle

It's not a Strategy Retreat; it's a Strategy Advance!

We don't call the annual strategic planning event a retreat; we use the term *Strategy Advance!* Our goal is to advance the strategy in line with the changing external customer, regulatory, competitive and global business conditions in such a way that we have the highest probability of succeeding in the marketplace. It's serious business, not just a cosmetic makeover.

Most annual strategy planning retreats are a dismal failure because they tend to make two very fundamental mistakes. The first is a backwards focused approach: review the results of the current strategy, decide to do better this coming year, add 10% onto the objectives, make a few new charts, and call it done. This approach avoids lots of meetings and 'messy' discussions. It also avoids the reality of the marketplace.

You can't drive a speeding car using the rear view mirror!

The second major mistake is to only involve the top executives, or worse yet, just the strategic planning department. A global charity dealing with sustainable water issues in underdeveloped countries didn't even involve the Board of Directors (who are recruited to be the external expert advisors) in discussing next year's strategy. The Executive Director and a few other staff added some new material and sent it to the Board for approval. And we wonder why strategy execution so often fails!

In our mind, the Annual Strategy Advance is a perfect time to really understand how well, or not so well, your company deals with execution issues. If you don't want to know, use one of the two safe approaches above.

He who knows 'why' will always win out over he who just knows 'what' and 'how!'

The most important questions during the Annual Strategy Advance begin with: "Why?"

- Why did we miss our goal in this region?
- Why did we beat out the competition in that region? Was it luck or a planned set of activities?
- Why are we struggling with employee engagement?
- Why did we lose those two customers?

These are excellent questions for a deep dive and we encourage the CEO to push hard on all the attendees to openly discuss and understand the whys.

And don't settle for external reasons that put the accountability outside the company.

- Why didn't we see it coming?
- Why didn't we react sooner?

These are not questions to place blame, but to deepen our understanding and develop real countermeasures so that it happens less and less in the future.

During the frantic pace of the business year as we scramble to deliver on day to day operations while also executing on the strategy, we don't often have the luxury of taking some quiet, reflective time to ask the important 'Why' questions.

The Annual Strategy Advance is a perfect time for reflection on internal organizational issues, as well as on market and competitive issues. If you did a proper job last year, your strategy is probably sound (barring any global financial meltdowns or disruptive technological surprises), but like most expensive and high-powered automobiles, is probably due for a tune up to check for wear and tear. The same principle applies to your strategy.

Every company has an annual planning cycle, which usually starts in Sept or October and culminates at year-end, when the next year's business and strategic objectives are established. Therefore the fourth quarter is an appropriate time to organize a 2-3 day Strategy Advance meeting and to advance your Strategy-on-a-Page Execution Roadmap for the next 12 months.

CONCLUSION,
BUT NOT THE END

Without the courage of leadership, we have nothing!

If you have made it through this guidebook from front to back then you have (hopefully) gained a few new insights about how to significantly raise the probability of successful strategy execution inside your organization. I also encourage you to explore the suggested reading in areas where you wish to gain further insight and understanding.

My objectives in writing the guide were multiple:

- To place a greater emphasis on execution
- To provide tools and techniques for more effective strategy development and execution
- To focus on the importance of leadership in the execution process
- To deliver insights and increased awareness on the role of CEO
- To urge you to action

- To make you think
- To make you smile and feel good about yourself and your leadership journey

Hopefully, at least a few of these goals were delivered.

Remember, strategy is realized through action: by getting your team aligned, your employees engaged, your initiatives underway and your products out into the market.

There is no strategy without execution,and there is no execution without leadership.

All the best on your journey to make a positive difference in your leadership role, wherever you find yourself.

John R. Childress

ACKNOWLEDGEMENTS

All I have done is put words on paper. The real authors of this guidebook are the many clients I have had the good fortune of getting to know through consulting assignments over the past several decades. There are too many to mention all of them, but I want to single out a few, since from them I learned the ins and outs of business leadership in a few short months of intense consulting assignments that otherwise would have taken me years of trial and error (mostly error I believe).

Lewis Booth, recently retired CFO of Ford Motor Company was a client twice, first as CEO of SAMCOR in South Africa and then as CEO of Ford of Europe. Lewis was a car man through and through, but above all he was deeply concerned about leadership team dynamics. He let us experiment on him, twice, and we refined our process under his guidance. Also our client mentors at Ford, John P. Fleming (now Global Head of Manufacturing) and David Schoch (now CEO, Ford of China) were both supportive and challenging.

The late John P. DesBarres, former CEO of TransCo Pipeline Company, had the courage to let me become an insider during the process of selling the company to a larger pipeline group. Very few outside the executive team or Board of Directors had such an inside look into such high-stakes business negotiations.

Ronald Burns, former President of Union Pacific Railroad Company, taught me about courage and making the right decisions for the right reasons. Ron resigned as President of Enron Pipeline Operations when Jeffrey Skilling took over the company and the 'energy trading silliness' started. Ron said: *"I don't care how high the stock price is, it's not good business!"*

Phillip Clark, President, and Dr. Robert Long, Chief Technical Officer, of GPU Nuclear for letting us work with their new management team following the Three-Mile Island Nuclear accident. It was there that I learned first-hand the power of corporate culture and how an unhealthy culture can lead to a business disaster, and then how a healthy culture can help get the company back on the right track.

Ian Walsh, former VP/GM of Lycoming Engines (now SVP/GM of Textron Defense Systems), showed us the importance of enthusiasm and an unwavering belief in people during a massive turnaround.

A special thank you to Gerry Giudici and Michael Mualem of AxleTech International and Stephen Elgin of General Dynamics Armaments. Also Joe Bione and Rich Pirrotta of The Whitehall Group. The journey continues.

Finally, Frank Tempesta, former President of Textron Systems Companies and Dick Millman, former President of Bell Helicopter, were clients for over 25 years, and taught me about leadership, the defense military industry, and the ins and outs of leading through boom and bust defense cycles.

There are also numerous consultants, staff and business partners who have pushed me to look for new approaches to solving the challenges of strategy execution. Most notably, Dr. Larry Senn,

Blackburne Costin, Rena Jordan, Michael McNally, Alan Hocking, Demetrie Comnas, Doug Kremer, and dozens of others too numerous to cite here. Thank you all for helping me develop myself, my skills, and ultimately the **FASTBREAK Strategy Execution** processes. And a special thank you to Alan Meekings for his thoughtful challenges on almost every principle, concept, and word!

And of course my wife and partner, Christiane Wuillamie, who not only improves my understanding of business realities, but also tolerates and even supports my travel and the long nights of proposal writing. A double "thank you!"

Alison Spence kindly did double duty to help edit and correct my grammar and poor spelling. Thank you.

My last dedication is to those of you who read this guidebook, who look with a critical eye at your own organizations, and who also choose to take a hard look in the mirror. If you decide to tackle the challenge of improved strategy execution, then I hope these thoughts and ideas will be of use.

I am a leader, therefore I lead;
I am an executive, therefore I execute;
I am a human being, therefore I care.

ABOUT THE AUTHOR

John R. Childress is a pioneer in the field of strategy execution, culture change, executive leadership and organization effectiveness, author of several books and numerous articles on leadership, an effective public speaker and workshop facilitator for bvoards and senior executive teams.

Career

Between 1974 and 1978 John was Vice President for Education and a senior workshop leader with PSI World, Inc. a public educational organization. In 1978 John co-founded The Senn-Delaney Leadership Consulting Group, the first international consulting firm to focus exclusively on culture change, leadership development and senior team alignment. Between 1978 and 2000 he served as its President and CEO. His work with senior leadership teams has included companies in crisis (GPU Nuclear – owner of the Three Mile Island Nuclear Plants following the accident), deregulated industries (natural gas pipelines, telecommunications and the breakup of The Bell Telephone Companies), mergers and acquisitions, and classic business turnaround scenarios with global organizations from the Fortune 500 and FTSE 250 ranks. He has designed and conducted leadership workshops in the US, UK, Europe, Middle East, Africa, China and Asia.

After retiring to France in 2001 John turned his hand to writing thriller novels. In 2004, he began to work again on consulting and coaching assignments where he subsequently developed much of the material and leadership processes used by The Principia Group in its work with senior executive teams on strategy execution.

Education/Interests

John was born in the Cascade Mountains of Oregon and eventually moved to Carmel Highlands, California during most of his business career. John is a Phi Beta Kappa scholar with a BA degree (Magna cum Laude) from the University of California, a Masters Degree from Harvard University and was a PhD candidate at the University of Hawaii before deciding on a career as a business entrepreneur in the mid-70s. In 1968-69, he attended the American University of Beirut and it was there that his interest in cultures, leadership and group dynamics began to take shape.

John currently resides in London and the South of France with his family and is an avid flyfisherman, with recent trips to the Amazon River, Tierra del Fuego, and Kamchatka in the far east of Russia. He is a trustee for Young Virtuosi, a foundation to support talented young musicians.

You can reach John at: john@johnrchildress.com

ABOUT THE PRINCIPIA GROUP

The Partners, Consultants and Staff at The Principia Group are dedicated to supporting CEOs and executive teams with robust business processes, management tools and consulting to deliver effective strategy execution, without an army of consultants.

> *You don't need an army of junior consultants running all over your company... but there is value in a senior 'business thinking' partner providing honest input, challenging your ideas, bringing new tools and approaches, assessing your team, working with you to build a better business.*
> *~ John R Childress, Founding Partner*

The Principia Group is a global consulting practice that believes no one knows more about a business than the people who run it. We are a global team of senior business executives with expertise in strategy deployment, organization design, leadership development, merger integration, culture change and performance improvement using an integrated methodology. We work closely with your senior team to build and implement business results, without an army of consultants. We like to think of ourselves as the consultancy that arrives without consultants.

The strength of The Principia Group is built on a commitment to rethinking the traditional, costly and invasive style of consulting so common today. Instead of armies of junior consultants descending on your company with the inevitable disenfranchisement of staff, we bring just two or three senior advisors with robust problem-solving methodologies who work alongside a selected group of your key people in building and implementing approaches that deliver targeted outcomes. As a result, our consulting engagements are cost effective and deliver sustainable business results. Because we systematically transfer our skills, tools and methodologies to your own designated people during the process your company becomes stronger and more agile – which in the end, is the only good reason for hiring consultants.

To learn more about The Principia Group, visit our website at www.theprincipiagroup.com or email us at info@theprincipiagroup.com

CITATIONS

1. Charan, Ram. "Why CEOs Fail." Fortune, June 1999.
2. Forbes. "The Reason CEOs Fail: An Update." *Forbes Magazine,* 22 April 2012.
3. Nohria, Nitin, et.al. *"What Really Works."* Harvard Business Review, July 2003.
4. Towers Perrin. *Closing the Engagement Gap: a Road Map for Driving Superior Business Performance.* Towers Perrin Global Workforce Study, 2007-8.
5. Bethune, Gordon and Scott Huler. *From Worst to First: Behind the Scenes of Continental's Remarkable Comeback.* New York: J. Wiley & Sons, 1998.
6. Hoffman, Bryce G. *An American Icon: Alan Mulally and the Fight to Save Ford Motor Company.* New York: Crown Business, 2012.
7. Minneapolis St. Paul Business Journal. *Select Comfort CEO Bill McLaughlin enjoys the Fruits of his Turnaround.* September 15, 2002.
8. Minneapolis St. Paul Business Journal. *Select Comfort tries New Strategies.* February 17, 2012.
9. Nadler, Mark. *Hard Part: Strategy Execution: Bridging the Gap between Vision and Action.* Oliver Wyman Journal, 2009.
10. Jamrog, Jay, et. al. *The Keys to Strategy Execution.* New York: American Management Association, 2007.
11. Merchant, Kenneth A. and Wim A. Van der Stede. *Management Control Systems: Performance Measurement, Evaluation and Incentives.* London: Pearson Education Ltd., 2007.
12. Lepsinger, Richard. *Closing the Execution Gap: How Great Leaders and Their Companies Get Results.* San Francisco: Jossey-Bass, 2010.

13. Lovallo, Dan and Olivier Sibony. *The Case for Behavioural Strategy*. McKinsey Quarterly, March 2010.

14. McKinsey & Company. *Improving Strategic Planning: A McKinsey Survey*. McKinsey Quarterly, September, 2006.

15. Smither, James and Manuel London (eds). *Performance Management: Putting Research into Action*. San Francisco: Jossey-Bass, 2009.

16. Mankins, Michael C. 'Stop Wasting Valuable Time." *Harvard Business Review*, September, 2004.

17. McKinsey & Company. *"Articles on Culture and Performance."* McKinsey Quarterly, No3, 2006.

18. Childress, John R. "Will it Make the Boat Go Faster?" *John R Childress, Rethinking Leadership*, Blog, 09 September 2011.

19. Kaplan, Robert S. and David P. Norton. *"The Balanced Scorecard - Measures that Drive Performance."* Harvard Business Review, January 1992.

20. Hutchins, David. *Hoshin Kanri: The Strategic Approach to Continuous Improvement*. England: Gower Publishing, 2008.

21. Wikipedia. *"Dr. Yoji Akao."* Wikipedia.

22. Smith, Greg. 'Why I am leaving Goldman Sachs." *The New York Times*, 14 March 2012.

23. Source: Thompson Database 2007.

24. Kennedy, John F. "A Special Address to Congress On the Importance of Space." 25 May 1961.

25. Engage Digital. 'Size of the "50 and over" Market: 100 Million People, Growing at 10,000 People A Day." 10 September 2012.

26. Enron Annual Report, "Enron Corporate Values." Enron Annual Report, Chicago: Chicago University Press, 1998, p73.

27. MSN Money Report. "Apple is the King of Retail Sales." *MSN Money Report*, 19 April 2012.

28. RadarSign. "How Effective Are Radar Speed Signs?" Data from ww.radarsign.com.

29. Zaleznik, Abraham. "Real Work." *Harvard Business Review*, Jan-Feb, 1989.

30. Katzenback, Jon and Douglas Smith. *The Wisdom of Teams: Creating the High-Performance Organization*. Harvard: Harvard Business Review Press, 1993.

31. Katzenback, Jon. *Teams at the Top*. Harvard: Harvard Business Review Press, 1998.

32. Childress, John R. and Larry E. Senn. *In the Eye of the Storm: Reengineering Corporate Culture*. Los Angeles: The Leadership Press, 1991.

33. United States Department of the Army. "Mission Command: Command and Control of Army Forces." *Field Manual No. 6-0*, Washington, D.C.: Headquarters, 2003.

34. Finkelstein, Sydney. *Why Smart Executives Fail: And What You Can Learn From Their Mistakes*. New York: Penguin, 2003.

35. Effective Crisis Management. *"The Tylenol Scandal 1982."* Effective Crisis Management: http://iml.jou.ufl.edu/projects/fall02/susi/index.htm

36. U.S. Government and National Commission on the BP Deepwater Horizon Oil Spill and Offshore Drilling. "Deep Water: The Gulf Oil Disaster and the Future of Offshore Drilling." *The Report of the National Commission on the BP Deepwater Horizon Oil Spill and Offshore Drilling*, 11 January 2011.

37. Balanced Scorecard Collaborative. *Survey of 143 Performance Management Professionals*. BSCol On-Line Community, March, 2006.

BIBLIOGRAPHY

Alanbrooke, Lord Field Marshall. *War Diaries 1939 – 1945*. California: University of California Press, 1998.

Bethune, Gordon and Scott Huler. *From Worst to First: Behind the Scenes of Continental's Remarkable Comeback*. New York: J. Wiley & Sons, 1998.

Bossidy, Larry, Ram Charan and Charles Burck. *Execution: The Discipline of Getting Things Done*. New York: Crown Business, 2002.

Charan, Ram and Geoffrey Colvin. "Why CEO'S Fail." *Fortune Magazine*, 21 June 1999.

Childress, John R. *A Time for Leadership: Global Perspectives from an Accelerated Market Place*. Los Angeles: The Leadership Press, 2000.

Childress, John R. and Larry E. Senn. *In the Eye of the Storm: Reengineering Corporate Culture*. Los Angeles: The Leadership Press, 1991.

Collins, James C. *Good to Great: How Some Companies Make the Leap . . . and Others Don't*. New York: Harper Collins, 2001.

Collins, James C. *How the Mighty Fall, And Why Some Companies Never Give In*. New York: Collins Business, 2009.

Collins, James C. and Jerry I. Porras. *Built to Last: Successful Habits of Visionary Companies*. New York: Harper Business, 2004.

Crawford, Fred and Ryan Matthews. *The Myth of Excellence: Why Great Companies Never Try to be Best at Everything*. New York: Crown Business, 2003.

Crowley, Michael and Ellen Domb. *Beyond Strategic Vision: Effective Corporate Action with Hoshin Planning*. New York: Butterworth-Heinemann, 1997.

Finkelstein, Sydney. *Why Smart Executives Fail: And What You Can Learn From Their Mistakes*. New York: Penguin 2003.

Hammer, Michael. "Reengineering Work: Don't Automate, Obliterate." *Harvard Business Review*, July-August 1990.

Hammer, Michael and James Champy. *Reengineering the Corporation: A Manifesto for Business Revolution.* New York: Harper Collins, 1993.

Hoffman, Bryce G. *An American Icon: Alan Mulally and the Fight to Save Ford Motor Company.* New York: Crown Business, 2012.

Hutchins, David. *Hoshin Kanri: The Strategic Approach to Continuous Improvement.* England: Gower Publishing, 2008.

Hsieh, Tony. *Delivering Happiness: A Path to Profits, Passion, and Purpose.* New York: Round Table Press, 2012.

Jacobs, Robert W., *Real-Time Strategic Change.* San Francisco: Berrett-Koehler, 1997.

Jamrog, Jay, et. al. *The Keys to Strategy Execution.* New York: American Management Association, 2007.

Johnson, Spencer. *Who Moved My Cheese?* New York: Putnam, 1998.

Kaplan, Robert S. and David P. Norton. "The Balanced Scorecard - Measures that Drive Performance." *Harvard Business Review,* January 1992.

Kaplan, Robert and David P. Norton. *The Execution Premium: Linking Strategy to Operations for Competitive Advantage.* Harvard: Harvard Business School Press, 2008.

Katzenback, Jon. *Teams at the Top.* Harvard: Harvard Business Review Press, 1998.

Katzenback, Jon and Douglas Smith. *The Wisdom of Teams: Creating the High-Performance Organization.* Harvard: Harvard Business Review Press, 1993.

Kotter, John P., and Holger Rathgeber. *Our Iceberg Is Melting: Changing and Succeeding Under Any Conditions.* New York: St. Martin's Press, 2005.

Lencioni, Patrick. *The Five Dysfunctions of a Team.* San Francisco: Jossey-Bass, 2002.

Lencioni, Patrick. *Death by Meeting: A Leadership Fable ... About Solving the Most Painful Problem in Business.* San Francisco: Jossey-Bass, 2004.

Lepsinger, Richard. *Closing the Execution Gap: How Great Leaders and Their Companies Get Results*. San Francisco: Jossey-Bass, 2010.

Leslie, Keith, Mark A. Loch and William Schaninger. *Managing Your Organization by the Evidence*. McKinsey Quarterly, August 2006, no.3.

Mcfarland, Lynn, Larry E. Senn and John R. Childress. *21st Century Leadership: Dialogues with 100 Top Leaders*. Los Angeles: The Leadership Press, 1997.

Merchant, Kenneth A. and Wim A. Van der Stede. *Management Control Systems: Performance Measurement, Evaluation and Incentives*. London: Pearson Education Ltd., 2007.

Mintzberg, Henry, Bruce Ahlstrand and Joseph B. Lampel. *Strategy Bites Back*. London: FT Prentice Hall, 2008.

Palmenter, David. *Key Performance Indicators: Developing, Implementing, and Using Winning KPIs* (2nd edition). New York: John Wiley & Sons, Inc, 2010.

Peters, Tom and Bill Waterman. *In Search of Excellence, Lessons from America's Best Run Companies*. New York: Warner Books, 1982.

Rumelt, Richard. *Good Strategy Bad Strategy: The Difference and Why It Matters*. New York: Crown Business, 2011.

Senn, Larry and John R. Childress. *The Secret of a Winning Culture: Building High-Performance Teams*. Los Angeles: The Leadership Press, 1999.

Smith, Paul. *Lead with a Story: A Guide to Crafting Business Narratives that Captivate, Convince, and Inspire*. AMACOM Press, 2010.

Smither, James and Manuel London (eds). *Performance Management: Putting Research into Action*. San Francisco: Jossey-Bass, 2009.

Tabrizi, Behnam. *Rapid Transformation: A 90-day Plan for Fast and Effective Change*. Boston: Harvard Business School Press, 2007.

Taylor, Carolyn. *Walking the Talk: Building a Culture for Success*. New York: Random House, 2005.

Welch, Jack and John A. Byrne. *Jack: Straight from the Gut*. New York: Warner Business Books, 2003.

Welch, Jack and Robert Slater. *Get Better or Get Beaten: 31 Leadership Secrets from GE's Jack Welch.* New York: McGraw-Hill, 2001.

Welch, Jack and Suzy Welch. *Winning.* New York: Harper Business, 2005.

PRINCIPIA ASSOCIATES

Also by John R. Childress

LEVERAGE: The CEO's Guide to Corporate Culture

A book specially written for the CEO and business leader to better understand what corporate culture is, why it matters, the impact on performance, where culture comes from, how to better understand the strengths and weaknesses of your own culture, and importantly, how to develop and sustain a high performance culture.

With over 35 years of experience advising CEOs and senior executive team of global organizations, international business consultant and author John R. Childress brings to life the important elements of corporate culture, including the role of leadership, approaches to culture change, culture myths, culture surveys and assessments and the role of culture in business performance and mergers & acquisitions.

The writing style is direct and to the point since CEOs and business leaders have little time to wade through consultant 'gobblygook' or academic text. **LEVERAGE** is also filled with examples and case studies that bring the topic of corporate culture to life!

You need to read this book before your CEO does!
- Frank Tempesta, former CEO, Textron Systems Companies.

This is the book every CEO has been waiting for! An insightful synthesis into the important topic of corporate culture, why it matters and how to separate the valuable from the B.S.
- Michael J. McNally, Aivia Corporation.

This book is both practical, insightful and honest in separating the facts from the fallacies about Corporate Culture.
- Demetrie Comnas, retired executive, J P Morgan Chase.

CPSIA information can be obtained at www.ICGtesting.com
Printed in the USA
LVOW05s2053111214

418359LV00013B/61/P